Pour _____ 'te,

Tu en a _____ autre
pays et _____ Sémé
en le lisam... ou _____ moins
en le parcourant...

Maman

The Spirit of

Languedoc-Roussillon

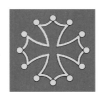

Barques catalanes, distinctive small regional sailing-boats.
Photo: © M. Castillo, Atelier des barques, Paulilles; courtesy Samuel Villevieille,
Conseil Général des Pyrénées-Orientales.

The Spirit of

Languedoc-Roussillon

Catherine Pinchetti

PACKARD PUBLISHING LIMITED

CHICHESTER

Dedication

To my students of French

To my mother

The Spirit of
LANGUEDOC-ROUSSILLON

First published in 2015 by Packard Publishing Limited, 14 Guilden Road, Chichester, West Sussex, PO19 7LA, UK.

ISBN 978 1 85341 152 6

Cover photos clockwise from top left by: Jean Giralt, Laurent Uroz, Mairie de Cucugnan, M. Castillo, Jean-Marc Favre, Catherine Pinchetti, Laurent Uroz & Jacques Miot.

Every effort has been made to attribute illustrations correctly, and to obtain permission to reproduce quotations and copyrightable extracts appearing in the text.

Prepared for Press by Michael Packard.

Design and layout by Hilite Design & Reprographics Ltd, Marchwood, Southampton, Hampshire, UK.

Printed in the United Kingdom by PublishPoint, KnowledgePoint Ltd, Winnersh, Reading, Berkshire.

Contents

Introduction

Languedoc-Roussillon was the cradle of Roman Gaul, and it spawned wine co-operatives and denim — the cloth 'de Nîmes' — the world's staple clothing material originally used to make jeans. It is the birthplace of the iconic French singers Charles Trenet, Georges Brassens, and of the poet Paul Valéry. Its coast is the western and southernmost half of mainland Mediterranean France, curving round towards Spain. A majestic river ending in a delta, the Rhône, and two mountain areas, southern Massif Central and eastern Pyrénées, form its natural boundaries. The oldest known European, Tautavel Man, made his home in this region.

You probably have bought some of its incredibly diverse wines, which are becoming more and more delicious with a very reasonable price tag. This is France's land of wine, collectively her largest, oldest vineyard and among the largest in the world. The sun and heat are no misers in Languedoc-Roussillon. Perhaps that is why you may be planning to try out its wide and safe sandy beaches, such as Gruissan and Argelès-sur-Mer; most of them were developed from swampy wastes by one of the most ambitious government projects ever launched. You may prefer to experience the thrill of sitting in a bullring, a hike to a vertiginous Cathar castle, the lazy beauty of a cruise along the Canal du Midi, sniff the robust aroma of a genuine Castelnaudary cassoulet or the sun-drenched fragrance of the local aperitif wines. Chances are you have at least seen pictures of the stunning arches of Roman Pont du Gard, of pink flamingoes in the Camargue salt marshes, of the walled city of Carcassonne and of snow-capped Mont Canigou emerging above pink cherry blossoms. Languedoc-Roussillon is all that and much more.

This book will not give you an exhaustive list of highlights. Original choices were made by my students of French, of various ages, horizons and nationalities, who demanded more than the acquisition of the language and the conventional background information. They wanted to gain insights into real French people, in their own words. In this book, Languedocians and Catalans from the past or present speak about their land through a selection of original extracts in French or Occitan offered with their English translation.

The story of Languedoc-Roussillon is a tale of contrasts. It is shaped like a vast amphitheatre stepping down to the sea in three tiers. The rugged, often ominous, mountains, the bony scrubland *garrigues* and the long sweep of coastline dotted with lagoons and salt pans or rocky coves near the Spanish border, are worlds apart. The bright sunshine can give way to ruinous flash floods. The shore concentrates the urban sprawl while the hinterland is sparsely populated: Lozère is known as the French desert. Montpellier, the regional capital which boasts the oldest Medical school in the Western world (12th century), enjoys a reputation of excellence in significant technologies and scientific research, but agriculture and services to the population remain the two basic sectors of the economy. The region may appear artificial because it consists of two distinct entities, Languedoc and small Roussillon — French Catalonia — but it is actually very strongly defined.

Two Romance languages other than French — Occitan, which gave its name to Languedoc, and Catalan — are still celebrated and, in the latter's case, spoken every day. Languedoc-Roussillon boasts a history of resistance. Its people have a long tradition of fighting against central governments. Roussillon resisted being swallowed by Spain but, once joined to France through royal marriage, it made sure its identity would be respected.

Languedoc wrote its history in the blood of its uprisings against northern French rule: the mass slaughter of its heretic Cathars, from nobility to peasants, forced it to become part of the Catholic kingdom in the thirteenth century; its indomitable Protestant Huguenots turned *Camisard* guerrilleros in the eighteenth century; the red swell of its angry winegrowers in 1907 engulfed the whole area in what was called the *Midi rouge* — leftist and trade-unionist 'Red South' — while among its Second World War *Résistants* rose emblematic Jean Moulin, a son of Béziers. Closer in time, feisty Georges Frêche, the late socialist Mayor of Montpellier and President of the region, was an indomitable crusader against Parisian bureaucrats. Today, the people of mountain towns and villages have been among the first in the country to say 'no' to shale-gas drilling, and their protests have been heeded.

Languedoc-Roussillon is proud of its cultural heritage and Mediterranean lifestyle. I once stood by the gate of the Romanesque Cathedral in Villeneuve-lès-Maguelone (Hérault), which sits on an islet in a lagoon: a group of young people clad in gold and red came, unfurled the old banner of Languedoc-Roussillon — the Occitan cross joined to the gold and red stripes of Catalonia — and engaged in a lively game of native *jeu de balle au tambourin*, very similar to modern squash. Their joy to be together and common pride shone through. Languedocians and Catalans have a passion for their traditional entertainments: bull-fighting — the *ferias* of Béziers and Nîmes are equal to their Spanish counterparts — and shows of horsemanship or nautical jousts, and a myriad of festivals celebrating their southern culture. One of the region's prestigious features, the Causses and Cévennes 'Mediterranean agro-cultural landscape' is on the UNESCO World Heritage List. Its historic heritage, from Roman monuments, Romanesque abbeys and churches, brightly painted Catalan boats, ruined castles of an obliterated civilisation to stern villages bravely huddled against the impenetrable Cévennes, can be admired across the region's five *départements*. So can the local rugby clubs, another southern passion, whose stars are Béziers, Montpellier, Narbonne, Perpignan or Quillan.

Modern Languedoc-Roussillon is the most attractive area in France. It is a national champion for demographic growth and the number of non-native residents, while immigration, mostly from North Africa, is high. Yet such popularity, combined with a chronic lack of industry, has bred economic and social difficulties. The region's fighting spirit, however, is unabashed and the pennant of its native riches, '*Sud de France*' ('South of France'), flies high.

Catherine Pinchetti

Acknowledgements

This book would not exist if it was not for my students of French: their enthusiasm and unflagging curiosity were the inspiration. My thanks go first to my editor, Michael Packard, for his patience and support, and for putting the manuscript on the right track. I have then to thank my husband, Don, who was always ready to test-read and offer comments, my daughters Sophie, for preliminary editing when needed, and Juliette, for her encouragement. Thanks, too, go to my friend, Patrick Gauthier, for his valuable suggestions; also to all the committed Languedoc-Roussillon *mairies, offices de tourisme*, associations, companies and individuals for their help and the warmth of their Occitan accents over the telephone; their names are listed at the end of the book.

CP

LANGUEDOC-ROUSSILLON

Muscat de Rivesaltes, a golden
apéritif or dessert wine.
Photo: Jean Giralt, Photothèque
Comité Interprofessionnel des
Vins du Roussillon (CIVR).

Map by Tim Aspden.

France's land of wine

Sun-drenched Languedoc-Roussillon consistently has the hottest and driest weather in France. Not surprisingly, its identity revolves around the growing of grapes and production of wine: it has become the largest wine-producing region in France and among the largest in the world. It kicks off the *vendanges* (grape-picking season) in late August.

The first grapes were planted here by the Greeks and the Etruscans from which, for 2600 years, the fortunes of men and wine have been inextricably entwined, though sometimes painfully. The winegrowers' riots in 1907 to defend their rights were ferociously repressed by central government. Languedoc-Roussillon used to be known as 'the fountain of table wines" but its huge output was of mediocre quality and largely consumed by working people — *le gros rouge qui tache* ('the coarse red wine which stains'). Yet it has come a long way during the last 25 years thanks to the skills and tenacity of men and women who are unlocking the potential of their extraordinarily diverse terrain. **Vins de pays d'Oc** now rank fourth in the world for wine exports and thrive on quality.

In Languedoc-Roussillon, schoolchildren learn all about wine early on:

En septembre ... après la rentrée scolaire ... plus d'une centaine d'enfants ont ramassé une quantité de raisins ... En octobre, les étiquettes pour cette cuvée ont été confectionnées en classe par les élèves ... [1]

In September, after coming back to school, over one hundred children picked a large quantity of grapes ... In October, the labels for this year's vintage were made in the classroom by the pupils ...

Some well-known Languedoc-Roussillon wines (from east to west) are **Tavel** and **Vins des Sables** (rosés), **Costières de Nîmes**, **Pic Saint-Loup**, **Coteaux du Languedoc**, **Picpoul de Pinet**, **Faugères**, **Saint-Chinian**, **Minervois**, **Cabardès**, **Malepère**, **La Clape**, **Fitou**, **Corbières**, **Maury**, **Côtes du Roussillon Villages**, **Collioure**. **Blanquette de Limoux**, originally produced by Benedictine monks, is the oldest sparkling wine in the world. The climate is ideally suited for Muscat wines — **Lunel, Frontignan, Mireval, Saint-Jean-de-Minervois, Rivesaltes** — while the fortified wines **Banyuls** and **Maury**, are a Roussillon speciality. Interestingly, the Languedoc-Roussillon vineyards were all established along the oldest Roman road in France, the *Via Domitia*, built in 120 BC to connect Italy and the Rhône valley with Spain; it is still visible in the heart of **Narbonne** (Aude).

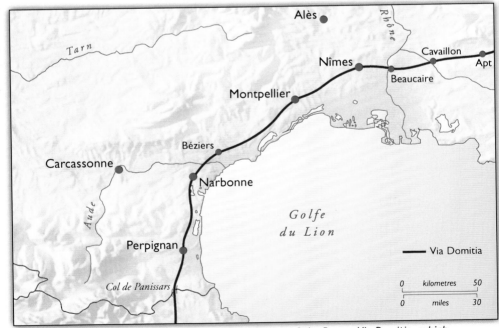

The route through modern Languedoc-Roussillon of the Roman Via Domitia, which linked Italy with Spain. Map: Tim Aspden.

The Entrepreneurial Spirit in the Languedocian vineyards

Gérard Bertrand was born in Narbonne (Aude) in 1965 and gave his name to a world-class brand of wines. He is a winegrower's son, but his first career was as a professional rugby player which ended in 1994 with a flourish, as captain of *Stade Fran*çais. Since then he has been building his wine 'empire', buying vineyards and châteaux thoughout the region. His bottles, which sport the deep red Occitan cross, are exported to 75 countries and earned him the coveted award of 'Red Wine Maker of the Year' in 2012. His autobiography, *Le vin à la belle étoile* (Editions de la Martinière) was published in 2015.

Le goût du vin, c'est Georges, son père, qui lui a transmis. Celui de la performance, c'est le sport ... Aujourd'hui, les vins du sud de la France ont une image. [2]

He was taught to love wine by his father, Georges. He was taught to win by sport ... Today, the wines of southern France have an image.

Gérard Bertrand, champion of southern French wines.
Note the variation of the Occitan cross, logo of Gérard Bertrand wines.
Photo: Vins Gérard Bertrand.

Jean-Claude Mas, the 'humble vintner', whose wines combine French subtlety with New World brio – one of his brands is called 'Arrogant Frog' – has vineyards in Montagnac (Hérault). His father's name, Paul Mas, appears on his wine bottles.

Son père était viticulteur ... mais entre une famille qui produisait de l'aramon à 300 hectolitres à l'hectare pour citernes de gros rouge ... et la réussite d'aujourd'hui, on parlera davantage de glissement tectonique que de fossé ... L'entreprise, avec une production de pas moins de trente cépages différents, en exporte la quasi-totalité, avec comme premier client le Japon ... A Montagnac, au milieu des vignes, Jean-Claude Mas a ouvert un restaurant avec un jeune chef japonais, Taïchi Megurikami, autour d'un concept, le luxe rural : Le jazz ... le pain qui se garde trois jours, la bonne cuisine, l'huile d'olive, le vin, le respect des racines, l'émotion par les sens. [3]

His father was a winegrower ... but between a family who produced 300 hectolitres per hectare from the *aramon* grape variety for coarse red wine tanks ... and today's success story, there is not just a gap but a tectonic shift ... The business, with a production using no fewer than 30 different grape varieties, revolves almost entirely around export, with Japan as its top customer ... In Montagnac, surrounded by vineyards, Jean-Claude Mas opened a restaurant with a young Japanese chef, Taïchi Megurikami. It is his interpretation of 'rural luxury': 'Jazz music ... bread which keeps for three days, good cooking, olive oil, wine, respect for one's roots, and emotion generated by the senses.

Marsanne and Carignan, less well known but typically Mediterranean grape varieties, used to make some Paul Mas wines. Photos: Domaines Paul Mas.

A strongly defined region

The long corridor between the Rhône valley and Spain, in the centre of the Mediterranean arc, is remarkable for its geographical, cultural and historical unity. However, **Languedoc-Roussillon** is a somewhat misleading name for the region, since it does not correspond to the former province of Languedoc but includes **Bas-Languedoc** (Lower Languedoc), **French Catalonia** (Roussillon) and sections of the **Massif Central** (Lozère). It matches more closely the ancient Visigoth territory of *Septimania*. The original Languedoc actually was the second largest province in France after Guyenne (Aquitaine today), the *lingua occitana* country: it stretched westwards to Higher Languedoc, with Toulouse as its historic capital, and northwards, with parts of the Rhône valley (Ardèche) and of contemporary Auvergne (Velay in Haute-Loire). Ties with the neighbouring Midi-Pyrénées region are steeped in history: for example, the Occitan cross is also called the Toulouse cross.

Bathed in the sunny but harsh Mediterranean climate, the area can be swept by fierce winds — *la tramontane, le grec* or *le marin* — or drowned by flash floods: the latter can be devastating in a city like Montpellier where paved surfaces tripled in twenty years and surface water drains off quickly. Languedoc-Roussillon's topography is curved like an amphitheatre facing the sea ranging from the flat and sandy shore — it shares the **Camargue**'s marshy Rhône delta with neighbouring Provence, dotted with brackish lagoons and salt pans — northern limestone plateaux covered with sparse vegetation (*les garrigues*), to the wild, rugged mountains from east to west, the **Cévennes, Causses, Corbières** and finally, the **Pyrénées** plunging into the sea at Roussillon's *Côte Vermeille*. The beautifully protected Regional Nature Parks —

Cévennes in Lozère, *Haut-Languedoc* shared between Hérault and Tarn in Midi-Pyrénées, *Narbonnaise en Méditerranée* in Aude, *Pyrénées catalanes* in Pyrénées-Orientales — and the heritage of the deserted hinterland contrast with the urban sprawl along the coastal plain: almost half of the region's 2 727 286 inhabitants are concentrated in the conurbation between **Montpellier** and **Nîmes** (INSEE, 2013).

Languedoc people are straightforward, friendly and fun-loving. Many can still speak the *Occitan* language of the medieval troubadours. It is said that:

> *...dans le Languedoc-Roussillon, l'Espagne pointe le bout de sa corne.*
>
> In Languedoc-Roussillon, Spain is showing the tip of its horn.[4] [i.e, feeling the Spanish influence, a bull-fighting allusion.]

They are avid fans of equestrian shows and bullfighting — there are over thirty *arènes* or bullrings across the region — and relish outdoor sports: besides *pétanque*, *jeu de balle au tambourin* — a close cousin of squash — there are nautical contests and water frolics (the ones at Sète and Agde are spectacular), and both rugby union and league.

The Roman amphitheatre at Nîmes.

A passion for bulls and horses

Nîmes and **Béziers** are both proud of their bullfighting schools. Nîmes is the place to go for Languedocian style *ferias*, bullfighting festivals: its monumental Roman Arena has seen many famous bullfighters. Béziers' *feria* is a strong rival, attracting over a million visitors during its five days. In Languedoc, though, no fun is complete without *les toros piscines*. You might wonder whether bulls actually have their own swimming pools there, but not quite! The sport involves running after a young bull in order to convince it to jump into a shallow pool which, unsurprisingly, is a delicate and sometimes dangerous task. In **Cap d'Agde**, the management of the local arena warns people:

> *La direction ne répond pas des accidents. Il faut être majeur pour descendre en piste.* [5]
>
> The management cannot be held responsible for accidents. Minors are not allowed into the arena.

Other popular bovine sports are *abrivado*, when bulls are let loose in streets and must be steered into the bullring by a group of riders, and *course camarguaise*, when young men compete to snatch cockades and strings tied to bulls' horns.

Bullfighting in France faces fierce opposition, of course. Among the objectors is the leading animal rights association *Trente millions d'amis* ('Thirty Million Friends') and *Comité Radicalement Anti-Corrida* (CRAC Europe). Nevertheless the sport was listed in 2012 in the Inventory of the Intangible Cultural French Heritage, for recognition by UNESCO. It is considered as *l'exception culturelle* (the cultural exception) of the *Midi* (southern France), more precisely the four regions of Languedoc-Roussillon, Provence-Alpes-Côte-d'Azur, Midi-Pyrénées and Aquitaine. Anti-corrida demonstrators argue that '*la torture n'est pas une culture*' ('Torture is not culture'). [6]

Herding bulls by a manadier.

Marking a bull by a razetteur.

This bull has the upper hand.

Photos by Laurent Uroz at the Manade de Grand Salan in Portiragnes (Hérault).

Cavalcades or *chevauchées* (horse shows) are obligatory in every local celebration throughout Languedoc-Roussillon. Music is provided by *peñas*, the neighbourhood brass bands.

A trio of gardians; *the rider on the right carries a long pike, as mentioned in the extract from* Catinat *by André Chamson, p. 74.*

An abrivado — the Provençal word means a swift action — is traditional in Languedocian festivals. Riders mount their Camargue horses in a triangular formation to steer bulls into the local arena while riding across town. Onlookers try to disrupt and scare the horses in order to let the bulls go free. Great skill is shown by the riders controlling the horses all the way to the bullring.

Photos: Laurent Uroz.

Water contests at Agde (Hérault). Photo : Laurent Uroz.

Languedocian water sports

> *Les joutes font partie intégrante de la culture et du patrimoine local ...*
> *Dans les tournois de joutes, vieux de plus de 400 ans, deux équipages*
> *s'affrontent. La barque des 'mariés' (la rouge) contre celle des 'jeunes*
> *hommes ou célibataires' (la bleue). Perchés sur le haut des barques, les*
> *jouteurs se battent en duel et tentent de renverser leur adversaire dans*
> *l'eau ...* [7]

Contests [jousts] are an essential part of the local culture and heritage ...
During tournaments, held for over 400 years, two crews, the married men
(red boat) and the young men or bachelors (blue boat) attack each other.
Perched on top of their boats, the contestants fight it out and try to make
their opponents fall into the water.

The badges of some Languedoc-Roussillon rugby clubs: (l to r) Béziers, Carcassonne, Montpellier, Narbonne, Perpignan.

Rugby clubs

Béziers, Carcassonne, Montpellier, Narbonne, Perpignan are now well known club names among European rugby fans.[8] Béziers celebrated its 100th anniversary in 2011 and is one of the most charismatic clubs in France, thanks to *'une succession de personnages hors du commun* ('a succession of extraordinary people'): Armand Vaquerin (1951-1993) alone won ten Brennus shields![9] Its rivalry with Narbonne regularly makes the headlines of the regional newspapers. The small town of Quillan in Aude is also outstanding for its repeated victories at national level. [The Brennus Shield - **Le bouclier de Brennus** - was created in the early 1900s by the Parisian master engraver and *'petit père du rugby français'* ('the Daddy of French rugby'), Charles Brennus (1859-1943). The large brass shield with a plaque on a wooden frame is awarded annually to the winners of the domestic French rugby union premier league.]

Languedoc-Roussillon, the rebellious

The area maintains its proud tradition of resistance against northern authority. No other region, except Brittany, was as quick to resist central (Parisian) governmental directives. In the Middle Ages, it was, with Midi-Pyrénées, the heartland of the Cathar sect which rebelled against the Pope in the name of purity and tolerance, and 'heretic' Languedoc had to be broken by destruction of its cities, slaughter and rape of its citizens: the population of Béziers was massacred in 1209 to the cry of *'Tuez-les tous, Dieu reconnaîtra les siens !'* ('Kill them all, God will recognize His own'!). Brought to its knees by the Catholic Church and soldiers from the north, it was forced to become a part of France in 1229. By the early eighteenth century, however, the Cathars' descendants had become Protestants and their fighting spirit endured against the atrocities of the armies of the 'Sun King', Louis XIV, the feared *dragonnades*. Not surprisingly, that spirit reignited against the German occupation during the Second World War with *'les résistants'*. Little Roussillon, wrenched from Spain in 1659, has shown the same indomitable spirit to keep its identity and Catalan language.

The Cathars continue to inspire esoteric books, witchcraft, tourist lore and very intellectual conferences and debates today (see the website www.chemins-cathares.eu). They thought the world was evil even though God was good, which meant that the world, including the (Catholic) Church, was evil too. Their aim, therefore, was to sever ties with the animate world, and their souls could be purified by God through successive reincarnations. The only stage of atonement for their sins was to become a Cathar after receiving the **Consolamentum**, the only sacrament they had, from *Parfaits*, the Cathar *'bonshommes'* and *'bonnes femmes'*, wise men and women learned in the faith. Their only prayer, since it came from Jesus, was the Lord's Prayer ('Our Father, which Art in Heaven' ...).[10] Here it is in the original Occitan:

> *La nostra paire qui es els cello, sanctificatz sia lo teus noms, avenga li teux regnes e sia faita tua voluntatz sico el ciel en la terra, e don a nos os lo nostre pa qui es sobre tota causa, e pardona a nos les nostres deutes aisico nos pardonan als nostre deutors, e nos non amenes en tentatio mais delivra nos de mal.*

Map of the Cathar territory. Map by Tim Aspden, source Pyrénées Magazine.

The 1907 winegrowers' revolt: the vignerons of St Thézan-des-Corbières (Aude) when even the women joined in. Photo: www.thezandescorbieres.com

Rebelling vignerons

In 1907, the winegrowers' revolt, triggered by a major slump in wine sales and the unfair competition of 'unnatural' wines, engulfed the whole *'Midi rouge'* ('Red South'), and encouraged socialist, or even communist ideas, out of character among predominantly conservative rural people: the government had to pass a law against fraud on food and drink, while the Languedocian winegrowers, after shedding their blood, were the first in France to create co-operatives to protect their livelihood.

Modern Languedoc-Roussillon

In 1962 the area became an attractive destination for *'rapatriés'*, the repatriated former French settlers from Algeria after the independence of that country, who often had a considerable experience in vineyards. Since the 1990s, Languedoc-Roussillon has remained a powerful magnet for other French people, and not least from elsewhere in Europe, either for higher education, permanent relocation, *résidences secondaires* or for retirement. It is also the sixth most attractive region for immigrants [the first five are Ile-de-France, Alsace, Provence-Côte-d'Azur, Corsica and Rhône-Alpes]. It is second only to Corsica for demographic growth, but holds the French record for the number of non-native residents, who settle overwhelmingly along the Mediterranean shore (3000 hours of sun per year), from Montpellier to Perpignan. Villages are left out by the demographic boom: in 2013, one out of four had fewer than 145 inhabitants!

Montpellier, the youthful regional capital, strong with its nearly 270 000 residents, is now the eighth largest French city with *Metropole* status, and is consistently rated among the finest for quality of life: to sip a drink in an outdoor café on Place de la Comédie in the middle of winter is not unusual! Languedoc-Roussillon, nevertheless, should not be mistaken for Paradise, because it is *'la région la plus pauvre de France derrière la Corse et devant le Nord'* ('France's poorest region after Corsica and above Nord—Pas-de-Calais') and shares with the latter the most severe unemployment rate in the *'Hexagon'* (i.e., Mainland France).

The reasons for this depressing statistic can be found in the climate: coastal-plain *Languedociens* were slaves to the hot and dry conditions and also, ironically, by the demands of the French market, to stick to the monoculture of wine, which killed off what little else there was. Retraining never existed, but the *vignerons* have been consistently exposed to the fluctuations of their industry. Those people who lived in the mountain valleys were always poor, or lost their livelihood when the coal mines and the silk industry vanished. But today, in this traditionally rural area, services, especially tourism, have developed quickly and the concentration of innovative and very small companies (***TPE, Très Petites Entreprises***) is the highest in France: **Outremer Yachting**, in **La Grande Motte** (Hérault), for example, started in 1984 and is today a world-class builder of catamarans. Yet, a great number of other companies do not survive for long, or conduct only strictly seasonal business. There are simply not enough jobs to absorb the influx of newcomers of working age. The poor road and railway networks in Languedoc-Roussillon only reinforce the imbalance between the coastal plain and the back country: the former has been a major passageway between Italy and Spain since the Roman period, but the latter, victim of its topography, depopulation and ensuing economic difficulties, is barely connected to the fast links, with the exception of the Carcassonne—Castelnaudary area towards Toulouse and the western edge of Lozère towards Clermont-Ferrand.

Georges Frêche, a stellar personality, pictured (left) as a Cathar martyr, holding an Occitan cross and resisting Paris to the last: (right) speaking with characteristic fervour in Narbonne in 2009. Credit: La Gazette de Montpellier, février 2010/ Internet.

Despite these problems, the land of sun and the red and gold *Occitane* cross is passionately proud of its main asset, the Mediterranean cultural heritage and lifestyle. The region's President and Mayor of Montpellier for 27 years, the socialist **Georges Frêche** (1938-2010), for example, launched a campaign far and wide — notably in China — and promoted Languedoc-Roussillon's finest qualities in 2006 under the brand *Sud de France*: its wines, made by 2800 winegrowers, its food products, and its maritime resorts, as well as wine tourism (see under the Gérard Bertrand logo, p. 5). One could also add its thermal-water tourism to the list, for Languedoc-Roussillon invested heavily in the rejuvenation of its 13 spas, such as **Avène** and **Balaruc** in Hérault, or **La Preste—Prats-de-Mollo** and **Molitg** in Pyrénées-Orientales.

Hot springs are a feature of the spas in Pyrénées-Orientales, such as here at Bains de Saint-Thomas. Photo: Syndicat mixte du Parc naturel régional des Pyrénées catalanes.

Promoting the region

Since 2006, the *'Total Festum'*, a major cultural event, has been organized by the Languedoc-Roussillon Region during the summer solstice.

> *Les civilisations occitane et catalane portent en elles le riche patrimoine des terroirs et des pays, de la culture, de la langue, de la littérature et de l'art ... mais aussi une certaine qualité de vie dont les maîtres mots sont: ouverture, accueil et intégration dans le respect de la différence.* [12]
>
> The foundation of Occitan and Catalan civilizations lies not only in the rich heritage of their diverse lands, their culture, their language, their literature and their arts ... but also in a special quality of life whose key words are: openness, hospitality and integration with respect for difference. [They call it *'convivéncia'*, enjoying life together.]

In the 2011 *Total Festum*, the programme (free except for the food) consisted of concerts, *'focs de la Sant Joan'* (bonfires), **'balétis'** (dance), street arts, traditional sports, **'sopar del terrador'** (banquets with regional dishes), and bilingual exhibitions revolving around the theme **'Catars e cruzada'** (Cathars and the Albigensian Crusade).

Promoting Montpellier

> *A Montpellier, la couleur attire la matière grise (hors Paris, 11,2% de la population active). Depuis toujours, la matière grise aime Montpellier. Elle aime son esprit d'entreprise et partage sa passion pour les hautes technologies, la recherche et les sciences du vivant ... Elle s'épanouit aussi grâce à ses étudiants, son soleil et sa Méditerranée.* [13] (Georges Frêche, président de Montpellier Agglomération)
>
> In Montpellier, colour attracts brains ('grey matter') (Paris excepted, 11.2% of the active population). Brains have always liked Montpellier. They like its entrepreneurial spirit and share its passion for high technology, research and life sciences ... They reach their full potential thanks to its university, its sun and Mediterranean Sea.

Mission Racine: the re-designing of the Languedoc-Roussillon shore

Leisure and tourism in Languedoc-Roussillon received backing from the national government in the 1960s to redevelop the previous swampy, mosquito-ridden and unexploited coastline of the *Golfe du Lion*: the aim was to compete against increasingly popular Spanish beaches and to offer millions of sun worshippers a cheaper, French Mediterranean alternative to the saturated and pricey Riviera. Seven high-capacity contemporary resorts and marinas, purpose-built by prominent architects — **Port-Camargue (Gard), La Grande Motte, Cap d'Agde (Hérault), Port-Gruissan, Port-Leucate (Aude), Canet-en-Roussillon, Port-Barcarès** and **Saint-Cyprien (Pyrénées-Orientales)** — were set amid new vegetation, thus complementing the 200km-long strip of ***Côte d'Améthyste*** beaches and the revamped seaside villages. It was a pharaonic project of the Gaullist era, that has been criticized, but its lasting legacy speaks for itself: the resorts have become towns, inhabited all year round.

In the twenty-first century, it is sustainable development away from the coast that promotes a different kind of tourism which enhances the legacy of those villages and small towns whose inhabitants doggedly shaped their inhospitable environment over the centuries.

Le Canet port and beach (Pyrénées-Orientales), examples of the remodelling of the region's shoreline. Photo: Ville de Canet-en-Roussillon.

The defence of the Occitan language

Les langues régionales, c'est notre patrimoine, notre passé et on ne peut pas avancer si on n'a pas les bases solides de notre passé. [11]

Regional languages are our heritage, our past. We cannot move forward unless we are solidly anchored in our past.

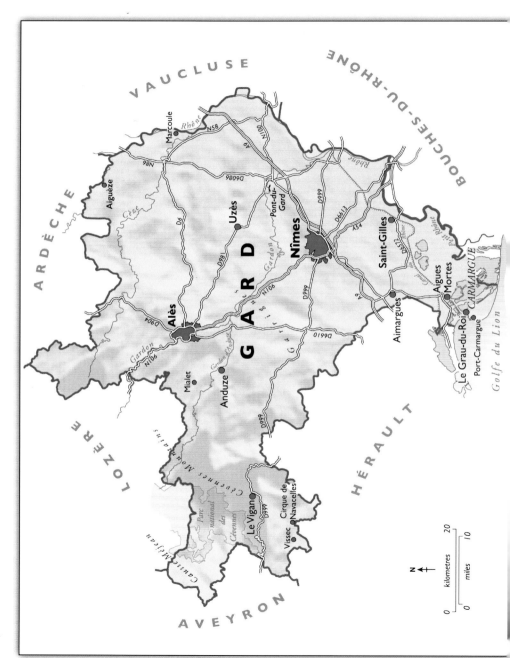

Map by Tim Aspden.

The five départements of Languedoc-Roussillon (from east to west)

Le Gard

This *département* faces the Rhône valley to the east and Provence beyond. The Romans built their most impressive French architectural structures in what was their first colony in Gaul, the province of *Narbonnaise*: the 49 metre-high aqueduct, the **Pont du Gard**, a Unesco World Heritage Site, and the exceptionally well-preserved monuments in the city of **Nîmes**, see p. 8. Here the local skill for cooking created **brandade de morue**, the smooth-as-silk mixture of salt cod and **Nîmoise** olive oil (only 'Boeotians' mix it with mashed potatoes!), decorated with the native **Picholine** olive variety.

The Pont-du-Gard aqueduct over the River Gardon, the boldest Roman monument in France (c. AD 50) which carried water from Fontaine d'Eure to Nîmes. The widest arch spans 24.5 m. Photo: Galen Frysinger, Bing Images.

Gard is the homeland of **Alphonse Daudet**, the author of the much-loved *Lettres de mon Moulin* — see p. 69, of the legendary trumpeter **Maurice André**, and of **Perrier**, the naturally sparkling mineral water in the club-shaped bottle.

The patrician grace of medieval **Uzès** is in sharp contrast with the stern memories of *'Le Désert'*, the secret assemblies of Protestants (*les Camisards*, so called because they all wore the same type of shirt) deep in the *Cévennes*.

The rugged, weather-beaten mountains, culminating at **Mont Aigoual**, 1565 m, are notorious for their épisodes cévenols (torrential thunderstorms). The area also had a coal-mining past, near **Alès**, which still employed 20,000 miners in the late 1940s and retains its own *Ecole des Mines*. **Anduze**, another Protestant stronghold, and its *Cévenole* valleys thrived for two hundred years, until the middle of the nineteenth century, on

Uzès: the 'Tour Fenestrelle' (42m) built in the Italian Lombard style, is all that is left of the 12th century Romanesque cathedral, partly destroyed during the Albigensian Crusade and in the 17th century during the Wars of Religion. Photo: Comité départemental du tourisme du Gard.

The village of Vissec (Gard) and gorges of the River Vis, near Cirque de Navacelles in the middle of the Causses.
Photo: Comité départemental du tourisme du Gard.

The temple in Anduze with its typical Protestant architecture. The stall to the left shows where modern priorities lie. Photo: Catherine Pinchetti.

the rearing of silk worms (*les magnaneries*) which fed on the leaves of mulberry trees planted on terraces built to retain a miserly mountain soil. It contributed to the prosperity of Nîmes, which used to be a world exporter of silk products: its hosiery (*bas à la péruvienne*) was worn by Latin American ladies, while its hard-wearing silk and cotton twill, originally for *Cévennes* shepherds, developed internationally as 'denim', thanks to the American businessman Levi Strauss (1829-1902), who used it for his 'jeans' work-trousers. Today, Gard is more attuned to cotton than silk, with the leading, but only surviving, male underwear company in France, **Eminence**, in **Aimargues**.

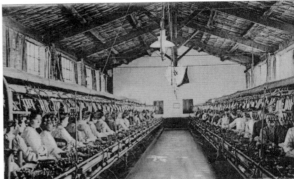

Old postcard photos of (above) the inside of a silk mill (filature), which employed an almost exclusively female workforce whose income would supplement the meagre existence of their farming menfolk; (left) the strenuous and unhealthy process of untangling the silkworm cocoons above barrels of boiling water ready for spinning. Photos: Archives municipales d'Alès (Gard).

Gard's once dynamic food-processing industry is in difficulties with the exception of **Royal Canin** — also in Aimargues — the pet food company, now part of the Mars Inc. group, founded by a local veterinarian. The only industrialized *département* in Languedoc-Roussillon, Gard now shares with its Rhône-Alpes neighbour in the lower Rhône valley, the fast-growing nuclear and pharmaceutical sectors. A speciality is developing in the dismantling of old nuclear plants, and the site at **Marcoule** is a pioneer in this field and a destination for work from other countries, such as Japan after the Fukushima disaster. On the coast, *Gardoise* beaches may not be as developed as others in the region, but **Port-Camargue**, created in the 1960s, is now the foremost yachting port in Europe.

Aigues-Mortes, salt of tears, salt of the sea

The citadel of **Aigues-Mortes** (1604m of fortifications), one of France's National Monuments, was built for the crusades by King Louis IX (Saint Louis, 1214-1270) and used to be directly connected to the sea. When the last Protestants were finally defeated in 1685, many of the men were sent to die in the galleys, while their women were imprisoned for the rest of their days in Aigues-Mortes' Constance Tower: in the prison registers, the entry of each of their deaths invariably mentions: '*Sa croyance est restée la même*'('Her faith remained unchanged').

The product of the city's salt marshes, *Salin d'Aigues-Mortes*, is no longer competitive in a global market for table salt, but retains its precious tradition. The main product nowadays is for *sel de déneigement* (salt for de-icing roads) and for agro-industry. The saltings attract wildlife and are a sanctuary for pink flamingoes. The coveted *fleur de sel*, the rare salt-flakes that form on the surface of the brine under certain wind conditions, are still harvested by hand and provide jobs for Languedocian *sauniers* (salt harvesters).

28

Sauniers at work and the prized 'fleur de sel'. Photos: Jean-Marc Favre, Groupe Salins.

Grand comme Paris, le Salin d'Aigues-Mortes est actif depuis l'Antiquité. Le labyrinthe de ses canaux, dont certains d'une surprenante couleur rose, surplombé par d'immenses tas de sel, forme un paysage unique. [14]

As large as Paris, *Salin d'Aigues-Mortes* has been exploited since Roman times. The maze of its canals, some of them of an astonishing pink colour [caused by tiny, carotin-rich algae], dominated by huge salt heaps, forms a unique landscape.

The Huguenot spirit lives on

Every year, Protestants from southern France (and elsewhere) gather at the *Assemblée du Désert*, near the *Musée du Désert*, in the village of **Mialet**. They sing *'La Cévenole'*, the Huguenot hymn to the memory of the *Camisards*:

Redites-nous, grottes profondes / L'écho de leurs chants d'autrefois /Et vous, torrents qui dans vos ondes /Emportiez le bruit de leurs voix /Les uns, traqués de cimes en cimes /En vrais lions surent lutter /D'autres- ceux-là furent sublimes /Surent mourir sans résister. [15]

Resound again, deep caves /With the echo of their hymns of yesteryear / And you, torrents which, in your waters /Would carry away the sound of their voices./Some, hunted from summit to summit /With a lion's heart knew how to fight. /Others and those were heroes /knew how to die without resisting'

Mialet, near Alès, is the birthplace of **Rolland** (**Pierre Laporte,** 1680-1704), one of those indomitable *Camisard* chieftains who led 3000 men to fight for freedom of conscience against 30 000 soldiers of Louis XIV, from 1702 to 1704.

Making money from memories!
Photo: Catherine Pinchetti.

Menu des Camisards
13,50 €

Salade des Camisards
Salade verte, Copeaux de Chèvres, Lardons, Croutons aillés
ou
Paté fin Cévenol
Artisanal avec Salade Verte
- - - - - - - - - - - - - -
Véritable Saucisse d'Anduze
Gillee et Garnie
ou
Andouilette Artisanale
Gillee et Garnie
- - - - - - - - - - - - - -
Moelleux à la Châtaigne
"Maison"
ou

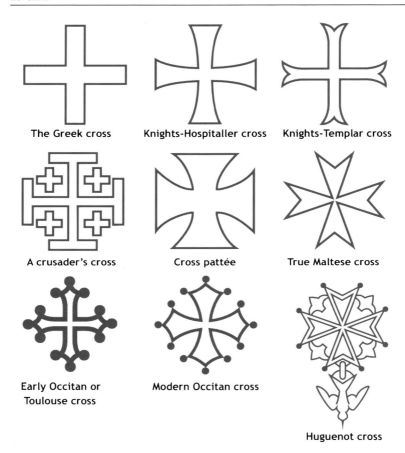

The Greek cross   Knights-Hospitaller cross   Knights-Templar cross

A crusader's cross   Cross pattée   True Maltese cross

Early Occitan or   Modern Occitan cross
Toulouse cross

Huguenot cross

The outlines of the many crosses derived and worn in the twelfth and thirteenth centuries; some were further adapted and used in modern times.

About crosses

The *croix occitane*, also known as the *croix de Toulouse*, or *croix du Languedoc*, featured on the heraldic shields of both Languedoc-Roussillon and Midi-Pyrénées, and is reputed to be of Visigothic origin because it can also be found in Spanish Catalonia and northern Italy [the kingdom of the Western Goths (Visigoths) encompassed much of south-western Europe]. Some claim it was a Cathar cross, but this is questionable because the Cathars rejected religious symbols. It is certain, however, that the Occitan cross first appeared on the seal of Count Raymond VI of Toulouse in 1211. It is curious, though, that the similar Huguenot cross also includes a flying dove pendant, which the Cathars also used.

These crosses, along with those of the medieval military orders after the first crusade (1099), the Maltese Order of the Knights-Hospitaller [of St John of Jerusalem], the Knights-Templar [of the Temple of Solomon – the Temple Mount] are all Greek crosses with 'arms' of equal length, in contrast to the Latin short and long-armed ones on which reputedly Christ was crucified. In heraldic terms, the Greek crosses are *'pattées'* (literally with feet), *'ancrées'* (like anchors) or *'cléchées'* (like keys). The *croix occitane* is both *cléchée* and *pommelée* (its ends bear little balls). There are 12 of those, three on each of the four arms, but it is unclear whether they symbolize the twelve months of the solar year — the four arms being the four seasons — or Christ with the 12 Apostles. Staunch Occitan partisans claim that the 12 balls should stand for the 12 départements allegedly comprising their former Occitan land.

The French Huguenots' cross, reputed to be designed by a Nîmes goldsmith after the Revocation of the Edict of Nantes (1685), bears some similarities with the Occitan cross and was worn essentially in the south of France until the nineteenth century. If you visit the site www.lavillerose.fr, an online jewellery store based in Toulouse, you will see that the cross is still very popular.

One other cross, derived from the Greek cross with four arms of equal length, is the Cross Pattée. It is widely used in awards, medals and insignia in many countries today, but unfortunately was adopted by the Nazis (the 'Iron Cross'), along with the Maltese Cross.

Playing pétanque in Anduze (Gard), and the badge of the Gardoise section the Fédération Française de Pétanque et de Jeu Provençal. Photos : Catherine Pinchetti.

Note the ubiquitous Occitan cross, even to dress up a pet dog. Photo : Catherine Pinchetti.

The Cévennes: stunning scenery for visitors, but harsh conditions for farmers. Photos: Catherine Pinchetti.

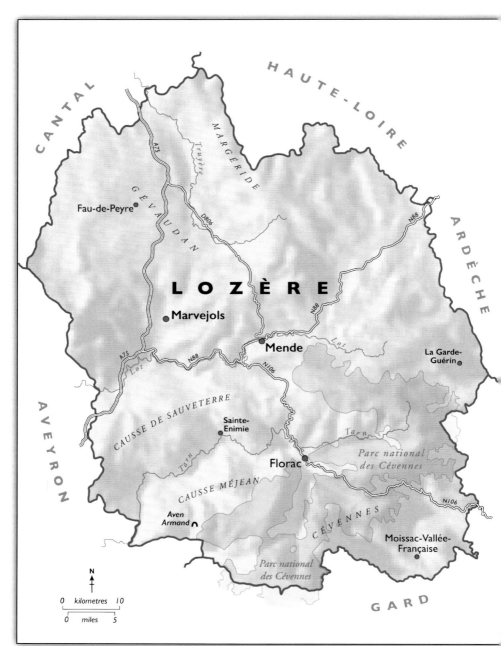

Map by Tim Aspden

The ominous dark mountains of Gévaudan where the 'beast' lurked. Photo: Catherine Pinchetti.

La Lozère

In the northern part of the region lies the 'French desert', the least populated *département* in France, where finding a doctor is getting more and more difficult these days. Lozère owes its name to its tallest mountain, **Mont Lozère** (1699 m). It is the only *département* in Languedoc-Roussillon that is land-locked. The country is remote, wild and unforgiving, with dark woods, arid moors and sharp mountain peaks. It was a place of legendary fear in the eighteenth century, threatened by a monstrous, wolf-like and forever mysterious *Bête du Gévaudan*. Few people ventured there up to the First World War, but its unspoilt nature and sparse population attracted French hippies, and later in the 1970s the first scientists began to study its ecology. It is now sought by *randonneurs* (hikers) and naturalists for its breath-taking scenery: the gorges of the River Tarn, *le Parc national des Cévennes* [a Unesco Biosphere Reserve reaching 1700m above sea level, accounting for 50% of the French species diversity, and the only national park in France to be fully populated by humans as well], or the lonely, cracked limestone steppes of the **Causses** — **Causse Méjean, Causse de Sauveterre** and **Causse Noir** — under which lies the giant cave of **Aven Armand**. The Causses encompass wide expanses of the neighbouring *départements* of Aveyron and Hérault as well. Both the Causses and the Cévennes have recently been awarded the prestigious status of a Unesco World Heritage site, as examples of a 'Mediterranean Agro-Pastoral Cultural Landscape' where nature and human activity coexist in harmony. The small round tangy cheese called **Pélardon**, typically Languedocian, is actually a Cévennes speciality, made from the raw milk of goats living with the local sheep.

Mende Cathedral and the statue to its builder (right) Pope Urbain V.
Photos: Catherine Pinchetti.

In contrast to the bleak *Causses* mountains is **Mende**, the more southern-looking city which is capital of the region. Its most illustrious son was the sixth Avignon Pope, Urbain V (1310-1370), born **Guillaume de Grimoard** in a tiny Gévaudan village, later becoming a powerful Bishop of Mende. After he rose to the papacy, he remembered his place of birth and ordered the building of Mende's Cathedral.

The town of Marvejols (Lozère), where the 'Bête de Gévaudan' is remembered.
Photo: Ethnovision.

La Bête du Gévaudan: A Still Unresolved Mystery

Ça a commencé en 1765. On est renseigné d'une façon précise par La Gazette de France, Le Courrier d'Avignon et bien des mémoires de cette époque. Mais cette bête, c'était quoi, au juste ? Un loup ? — Non. A dire vrai, on ne sait pas trop. D'après l'un, c'était un animal à la fois chien et hyène, qui aurait été amené en France par des pirates barbaresques. D'après un autre ... c'était une bête de la taille d'un veau, au corps rougeâtre, avec d'énormes griffes et d'énormes crocs, une raie noire sur le dos et des oreilles pointues, droites comme des cornes — Et il y a eu beaucoup de victimes ? — Des dizaines et des dizaines. Dans toute la Margeride, et au nord..., et au sud, vers Mende ... Et à Saint-Chély, même, un petit berger a été attaqué sur un plateau. Pour échapper à la bête, il a sauté du haut de la falaise. C'est ça, 'Le Saut du Berger'— Incroyable. Et où cette bête pouvait-elle se cacher ? — Mais partout ... Notre Margeride est un pays de caches, de grottes ... inaccessibles ... Partout, des montagnes en vagues serrées, comme un immense moutonnement de granit, de pierrailles, de pentes ... de grands espaces déserts. Peu de routes. Vous comprenez pourquoi, de tous temps, il y a eu, par ici, des brigands, des fuyards, des déserteurs, des Camisards, des maquisards, des traqueurs et des traqués ... Oui, c'est un beau pays de violence et de sang. [16]

The Bête du Gévaudan still lurks in Marvejols (Lozère)! The statue was inspired by the various depictions of an animal imagined by many people. Photo: Mairie de Marvejols.

It all started in 1765. We have precise accounts given by *La Gazette de France, Le Courrier d'Avignon* and many memoirs of that time. But that beast, what was it, exactly? A wolf? — No. To tell the truth, nobody knows for certain. One would say it was a cross between a dog and a hyena, which would have been brought to France by Barbary pirates. Another one would claim it was a beast the size of a calf, with a reddish body, enormous claws and fangs, a black stripe on its back and pointy ears standing up like horns.—And there were many victims? — Scores and scores. All over *Margeride*, and to the north ... and to the south, near Mende ... In Saint-Chély, even, a young shepherd was attacked on a plateau. To escape from the animal, he jumped over the cliff. That is the origin of *'le Saut du Berger'* ('Shepherd's Jump') — Unbelievable. Where was that beast hiding? — But everywhere. Our *Margeride* is a land of hiding places, caves ... inaccessible ... Everywhere, waves upon waves of mountains, like a huge swell of granite, rocks, slopes ... a desert wasteland. Few roads. You understand why, from the beginning of time, this was the country of highwaymen, fugitives, deserters, *Camisards, maquisards* (French *Résistants*), pursuers and pursued ones. Yes, it is a beautiful place of violence and blood.

Until June 1767, over 100 people were attacked and the majority did not survive. A local peasant, Jean Chastel, finally killed something which resembled a large dog. However, descriptions insisted that the animal was of an unknown species. Since some victims were decapitated or left naked, the attacks could have been made either by a man, disguised as a beast, or an animal trained to kill by a psychopath.

Du monde pour le 14 juillet ! (Rocles, Lozère)

Il y a bien longtemps qu'il n'y avait pas eu autant de monde dans les rues du village pour un 14 juillet ... Pour la pétanque, il n'y avait pas assez de place pour tous et les résidences secondaires étaient pratiquement toutes ouvertes. Quel changement avec nos mois d'hiver où l'on ne voit pas un chat ! Les fêtes du pain, les grillades et le cochon grillé font le plein. [17]

Company for Bastille Day!

It has been years since we last saw so many people in the village streets for a Bastille Day ... For *pétanque*, there was not enough room for everybody, and the holiday homes were almost all open. What a change, compared with our winter months when we don't get to see a single soul! The Bread Festivals, the barbecues and the hog roast were hugely popular.

Fêtes du Pain are indeed among Lozère's traditions. In this pastoral land, where the inhabitants lived in severely isolated villages, bread for each family was made at home once a month and brought to be baked in the common village oven — the loaves bore the mark of their owners. Today, bread is delivered to the still isolated villages by bakers' vans, but many village ovens have been proudly restored by the citizens as local heritage. *Fêtes du Pain*, organized by *mairies*, are happy occasions which aim to strengthen social bonds: a new volunteer every year takes on the responsibility of baking the loaves made by residents, associations and schoolchildren, which are then shared during a village lunch.

ête du Pain at Fau-de-Peyre: the bread oven, the prepared and baked loaves, and eating the read. Photos: Daniel Mantrand, Maire de Fau-de-Peyre (Lozère).

Digital Age in Lozère

Digital Age communication technologies could break the isolation of rural Lozère. *POLEN, Pôle lozérien d'Economie Numérique* (Lozère's hub for digital economy) was created in 2004 in partnership with the *Conseil général* (local government) of the *département* to foster the establishment of e-businesses and attract incomers, thanks to the development of *télétravail* (work from home). Some POLEN slogans were:

> *En Lozère, votre entreprise respire.*
> (In Lozère, your company can breathe.)
>
> *Faites pousser vos idées.* (Make your ideas grow.)
>
> *Sortez de la meute, la Lozère sourit aux jeunes loups!*
> (Stand out from the pack, Lozère smiles on young wolves!) [A playful reference to the area's dreaded wild animals.][18]

Le Maquis 'Montaigne': Cévennes' resistance hotbed

Near **Col de l'Exil** (Exile Pass, so called because it was the last place where local Huguenot families could say farewell to their male loved ones off to the galleys for refusing to convert to Catholicism) and the village of **Moissac-Vallée Française**, a commemorative stone stands in memory of the French, German (Communists), Spanish (Republicans) and other Europeans who fell fighting for freedom against the Nazis in 1944. It also pays tribute to those *Cévenole* mountains, ravaged by *dragonnades* after 1685, which continued to be *'une terre de refuge et d'accueil, avec sa population dont la propre histoire est marquée par la défense de la liberté de conscience'* ('a land providing refuge and shelter, with its population whose own history is a long battle for the defence of freedom of conscience and ideas.').[19]

The Cévennes. Photo: Catherine Pinchetti.

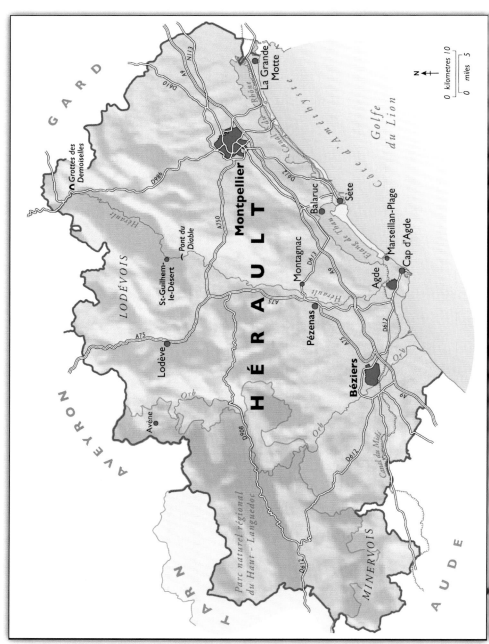

Map by Tim Aspden

L'Hérault and l'Aude

These are the two biggest wine-producing areas in France. **Aude** actually boasts the largest co-operative group in the country, which is now an international leader in the sector of varietal wines, *Val d'Orbieu-Uccoar*. Wine, however is not the only wealth.

Hérault has four treasures: the ancient Medical School of the **University of Montpellier**, the oldest in the Western world; the unconventional poet-singer **Georges Brassens** (1921-1981), whose bushy moustache and earthy, provocative voice dominated the French airwaves in the 1950s; the poet, philosopher and Academician **Paul Valéry** (1871-1945), today admired in countries as distant as Japan; and the **Bouzigue oysters**, cultivated in the salt waters of *Étang (Lake) Thau*, coveted to the point of being frequently stolen in the dead of night! If every road seems eventually to lead to a vineyard, it is not without going through mountains (*Causses, Cévennes, Haut-Languedoc*), past spectacular caves (*Grotte des Demoiselles)*, lagoons and sandbars or, as in Gard (**Saint-Gilles-du-Gard**), Unesco World Heritage Sites along the *Via Tolosana* to Santiago de Compostela (**Saint-Guilhem-le-Désert**). The little town of **Pézenas**, *'le petit Versailles du Languedoc'*, lives off the memory of Jean-Baptiste Poquelin, *nom de plume* of the great **Molière** (1622-1673), who wrote his first comedies there for the fabulously rich theatrical enthusiast, the Prince de Conti: its summer street festival *'Molière dans tous ses éclats'* would certainly not be disowned by the 'patron saint' of the French language. Another little town, **Lodève**, turned away from mining and hopped on the culture train, inviting Mediterranean countries every year to its poetry festival, *Voix de la Méditerranée*. **Béziers** prides itself as the birth-place of the famous *Résistant* leader, **Jean Moulin** (1899-1943); the 'French Sevilla' also has its native matador, **Sébastien Castella** (born in 1983).

Georges Brassens with his pipe and one of his cats — always called 'le chat' — giving him a dose of the unfettered feline love he cherished. Photo: babelio.com

To be buried with love in Sète

Sète, with its 12-km long beach and **Etang de Thau**, France's largest saltwater lake, looks like an island and earned the name of 'Languedocian Venice'. Sète's two famous sons, **Paul Valéry** and **Georges Brassens**, both had the same ultimate wish: to be buried in their native city, in sight of the blue Mediterranean. Valéry wrote the poem *'Cimetière marin'* and Brassens the song *'Supplique pour être enterré sur une plage de Sète'* ('Plea to be buried in a Sète beach').

Paul Valéry was a true son of the Mediterranean of which he was intensely proud. His father was a Corsican customs officer and his mother hailed from Genoa. Although born in Sète, he grew up and was educated in Montpellier studying law at the University. He wrote about his native Sète :

> *Je suis né dans un de ces lieux où j'aurais aimé de naître. Je me félicite d'être né en un point tel que mes premières impressions aient été celles que l'on reçoit face à la mer et au milieu de l'activité des hommes ... Rien ne m'a plus formé, plus imprégné, mieux instruit − ou construit − que ces heures dérobées à l'étude ... mais vouées dans le fond au culte inconscient de trois ou quatre déités incontestables : la Mer, le Ciel, le Soleil.* [20]

I was born in one of those places where I would have liked to be born. I am very grateful I was born in a place where my first impressions originated both from the sea and the activity of men ... The building-blocks of what I was to become were three or four determining deities, the Sea, the Sky, the Sun, whom I unconsciously worshipped during those supremely formative hours stolen from my studies.

He moved to Paris when a young man, writing poetry which was influenced by the symbolist poet Stephane Mallarmé. In 1897 he gave up writing completely and kept himself by working for the Department of War and later for the chief officer of the Havas News Agency, while immersing himself in mathematics and physics, and setting out his thoughts in the 26 000 pages of his *Cahiers* (1894-1914). But it was his friend, the writer André Gide, who encouraged him to return to poetry. He wrote *La Jeune Parque* ('The Young Fate') in 1917, *Le Cimetière Marin* ('The Graveyard by the Sea') in 1920 and *Charmes* ('Charms') in 1922 to great acclaim. He was accorded the status of 'national poet', appointed Professor of *Poétique* at the prestigious Collège de France and elected to the Académie Française. When he died in 1945, he was honoured with a state funeral.

Valéry was a man of strong principles and great intellect who explored the nature of thought, the depths of literary consciousness and its relationship with language, and was a founding father of analytical literary criticism taken over by the linguistic Structuralists. All his prose texts (speeches, lectures, essays and forewords) are published under the title *Variétés*. He is a difficult author to read and understand and, unsurprisingly, his thoughts are favoured by French philosophy students for dissertations. His more accessible short book is *Soirée avec Monsieur Teste; Teste* (the mind) being his *alter ego*.

A heritage shaped by terroir

Pézenas' tempting little pasties — *les petits pâtés de Pézenas*

In **Pézenas**, an Hérault culinary speciality dating from the late eighteenth century is the hors d'oeuvre of cotton-reel-shaped sweet and savoury pasties with a lamb, lemon, spices and sugar filling. They were actually created by the Indian cook of Lord Robert Clive, British Viceroy of India at that time, who enjoyed staying in Pézenas whenever he needed treatment at the Montpellier Medical School. To show the locals his appreciation, he authorized his cook to divulge the recipe!

The famous pasties of Pézenas. Photo : © Pierre Ramond, courtesy Office de Tourisme de Pézenas—Val-d'Hérault.

Forgotten grapevine varieties have a future

Marseillan is a picturesque Languedocian coastal village in Hérault, with a very long beach. It is home to the archive of grapevine varieties which is unique in the world: the *Domaine de Vassal / Centre de ressources génétiques de la vigne* supervised by INRA, the French National Institute of Agricultural Research. [21] It stores some 7500 vine genotypes, and is a leader in the conservation, study and development of grapevine biodiversity.[21 & 22] A fair number of Languedoc-Roussillon *vignerons* are keen to revive the ancient, rustic grape varieties ideally suited to their parcels of land (and see Gérard Bertrand and Jean-Claude Mas on pp. 5 & 6). Marseillan also happens to be the home of **Noilly-Prat** vermouth, founded in 1813.

The Canal du Midi pound at Castelnaudary. Photos: Audrey Duval.

Canal du Midi — Tour de force

The canal reaches 189 metres above sea level at its highest point at **Seuil (Col) de Naurouze** (on the border of Haute-Garonne and Aude) west of Castelnaudary, where the natural flow of water is westwards to Toulouse or east to the Mediterranean. In Béziers, the seven successive ***Fonserannes*** locks ascend 21 metres, and are still operated in the original way, now letting through 10 000 boats a year. [23]

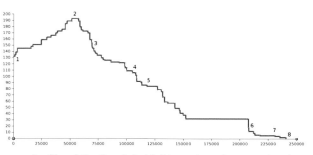

Profile of the Canal du Midi in metres above sea level, from 1 (at Toulouse), 2 (Seuil de Naurouze), 3 (Castelnaudary), 4 (Carcassonne), 5 (Trèbes), 6 (Béziers, Fonserannes Locks), 7 (Agde), 8 (Sète). Source: Wikipedia.

The Fonserannes locks at Béziers. Photo: staircase_ sm/sydneyventureslle.com

The fertile **Lauragais** was an important wheat-growing area. Grain and flour from its 32 wind-mills, which benefited from the westerly and southerly winds in the natural gap between mountainous Haut-Languedoc and Montagne Noire, were transported in barges along the canal. These buildings fell into disrepair, but the remaining **Moulin de Cugarel,** located on a hill just outside Castelnaudary and fully restored in 1969, is the only one now open to visitors.

The restored Moulin de Cugarel. Photo: Audrey Duval.

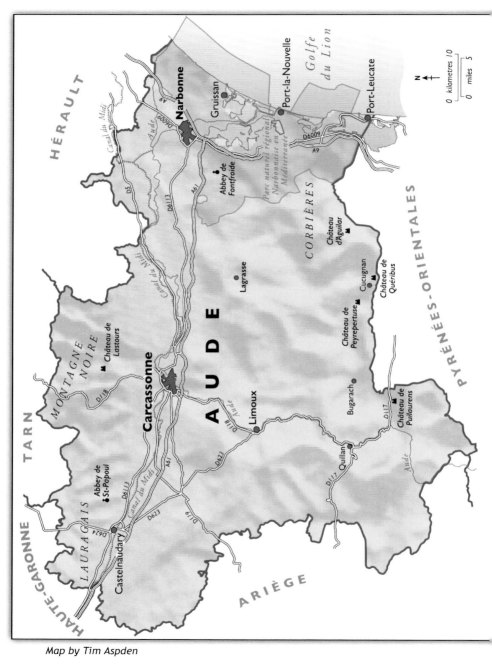

Map by Tim Aspden

L'Aude

The *département* retains an air of mystery, perhaps because one of its tiny villages, **Bugarach** (200 residents), was supposed to be spared, according to a Mayan prophecy, by the Apocalypse predicted for 21 December 2012. Actually, it is part of *le Pays Cathare* ('land of the **Cathar**s') — see p. 15, where the vertiginous ruins of their castles — **Aguilar, Lastours, Peyrepertuse, Puilaurens, Quéribus** and ten other *'châteaux du vertige'*— clung to the rocky hilltops of eerie **Hautes-Corbières** and witnessed the devastation of the Occitan country during the Albigensian Crusade (1209-1229) followed by the Dominican Inquisition in the fourteenth century. A native *Audois* and the last-known Cathar *parfait* — a holy person who could give the only sacrament of the faith, the *Consolamentum*, and who had the privilege of 'ordaining' new *parfaits* — was burned at the

The Cathar castle of Quéribus, mostly destroyed in the Albigensian Crusade, but rebuilt in the 17th century. Photo: Mairie de Cucugnan.

stake in **Villerouge-Termenès**: the death of **Guilhem Bélibaste** (1280?-1321) also brought about the end of the southern Cathar Church. A hiking trail, *Le Sentier cathare*, now runs through this land of tragic legends, from **Port-La Nouvelle** to **Foix** (Ariège in the Midi-Pyrénées region). The uncompromising supremacy of the Catholic Church underlines the high number of abbeys in Aude, such as **Fontfroide** or **Saint-Papoul**.

Carcassonne. Photo: Bing images.

The medieval fortified city of **Carcassonne** — 52 towers, two rings of walls and three kilometres of battlements — is a Unesco World Heritage site which attracts over two million visitors a year. Stunningly illuminated every Bastille Day, Carcassonne is home to the *Centre d'Etudes cathares*. Aude, however, holds more in store than the Cathars and its vineyards cascading down to the sea. Its contrasted landscapes range from the first Pyrenean mountains (*Pyrénées Audoises*) in the south-western corner, the rolling and generous countryside of *Lauragais*, on the road to Toulouse, the tormented *Corbières* (culminating at *Pech de Bugarach*, 1231 m) with their gorges and caves, to the deep forests of *Montagne Noire* near Carcassonne and the vast expanse of lagoons forming the *Parc naturel régional Narbonnaise en Méditerranée*.

Charles Trenet, a portrait to accompany the music of the song, Douce France. Photo: Guenael, greatsong.net.

An iconic French character hails from these parts: a son of Roman Narbonne, the legendary fair-haired and blue-eyed singer with the baby face, **Charles Trenet** (1913-2001), whose cheerful tunes were translated and adapted all over the world — see p. 76. On the culinary front is the *cassoulet* of **Castelnaudary**, a hearty bean, pork and goose or duck *confit* casserole, baked for hours in a sandstone pot called a '*cassolo*'; the town pays it homage in August with its *Fête du Cassoulet* (next page). If olives are less famous, they are nonetheless another pride of Aude, with its olive growers' cooperative, **L'Oulibo** (founded in 1942): Languedoc-Roussillon, the first French producer of table olives and the second of olive oil, owes a great deal to it.

A communal meal during the Fête du Cassoulet at Castelnaudary.
Photo: Didier Rumeau.

Gruissan, an example of a *'circulade'* village in Aude

Like several Languedocian villages by the sea, old Gruissan was
built like a snail shell: its streets are all circular, winding around
the watch tower in concentric circles, a good defence strategy
against North African pirates. Its identity has been preserved,
next to the modern **Gruissan-Port** and the popular resort of
Gruissan-Plage. [24]

The circulade village of old Gruissan. Photo: Bing images.

'La Première bulle' in Limoux — The first 'bubbly' in Limoux

L'abbaye bénédictine fondée à la fin du 8ème siècle abrite un chef-d'oeuvre de la sculpture romane en marbre blanc des Pyrénées ... Mais c'est bien dans les celliers, à une température constante de 15°C que les moines trouvèrent, par hasard, la première bulle. Celle qui depuis 1560 fait le succès de la Blanquette de Limoux. [25]

The Benedictine abbey [Saint-Hilaire] founded at the end of the eighth century holds a masterpiece of Romanesque sculpture in white Pyrenean marble ... However, it is in the cellars, whose temperature remains constant at 15°C, that the monks discovered, by chance, the first bubble. Since 1560 it has been the best kept secret of *Blanquette de Limoux* sparkling wine.

Limoux, in *Pays Cathare,* is also known for its ten-week long winter carnival and its ***Toques et Clochers* Festival,** held every Palm Sunday weekend: the auction sale of wines from the different vineyards of Limoux *terroir* helps fund the restoration of the local church.

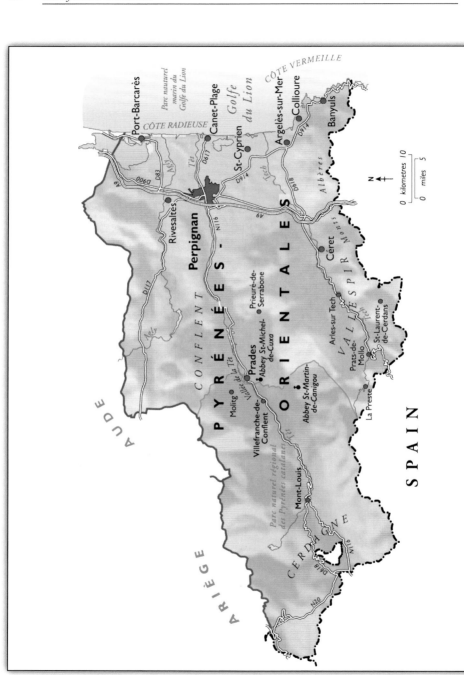

Map by Tim Aspden.

Les Pyrénées-Orientales

The identity of Roussillon

The old province of **Roussillon** is home to French Catalans. When it was ceded to France under the terms of the Pyrénées Treaty of 1659, the young King Louis XIV also acquired a bride in the bargain, Infanta Maria-Theresa of Spain, and the eastern border between Spain and France was finally settled: Marshal Vauban's fortifications of **Mont-Louis** and **Villefranche-de-Conflent** (Fort Libéria), listed as Unesco World Heritage Sites, made sure of that.

Pyrénées-Orientales is bordered by mountains: the stunning **Parc naturel régional des Pyrénées catalanes** to the west — a quarter of the *département* — culminating in *Pic Carlit* (2931 m) and snow-capped *Mont Canigou* (2785 m), the *Corbières* to the north and the *Albères*, the last Pyrenean massif before the

Part of Vauban's fortifications at Mont-Louis with the snowy mountains as a backdrop. Photo: Syndicat mixte du Parc naturel régional des Pyrénées catalanes.

Mediterranean by the Spanish border. Their natural beauty is as diverse as high mountain *Capcir*, French *Cerdagne* and upper *Conflent* (the upper valley of the Têt river), the lush slopes of lower *Conflent* and *Vallespir* (the Tech valley), the sweeping sandy beaches (**Canet, Argelès-sur-Mer**) of *Côte Radieuse* or the rocky coves (**Collioure, Paulilles**) of Côte Vermeille. Outdoor pursuits range from skiing (**Font-Romeu**) and hiking to nautical sports: *Sentier sous-marin* (Underwater Trail) between **Banyuls** and **Cerbère** is a snorkelling experience while *Parc Naturel marin du Golfe du Lion* protects a rich marine biodiversity along a 100 km-long shore. With 320 days of sunshine per year and the southernmost towns in France, Pyrénées-Orientales is famous for the vibrant colours of its landscape enhanced by the almond, apricot, cherry and peach orchards and a wide variety of southern vegetables that ripen next to carefully terraced vineyards. The cherries grown in **Céret** have the privilege to be chosen for the French President's table.

It is hardly surprising that the oldest European ever discovered, the *Tautavel* man, lived there some 500 000 years ago.

Roussillon inspired many painters — Matisse, Derain, Soutine, Juan Grís, Picasso and Salvador Dalí, who immortalized Perpignan railway station and believed it to be '*el centre del món*', 'the centre of the world'. Its villages welcomed Spanish Catalan refugee artists and intellectuals during the Spanish Civil War: **Céret** was a Cubist hotbed and is proud of its *Musée d'Art moderne*. **Prades** owes its international reputation to the cellist **Pablo Casals** (1876-1973), who created the chamber-music festival bearing its name in 1950. **Rivesaltes** is the birthplace of the sculptor **Aristide Maillol** (1861-1944).

The Abbey of Saint-Martin-de-Canigou.
Photo: Parc naturel régional des Pyrénées catalanes.

Pyrénées-Orientales is also endowed with a remarkable architectural and cultural heritage: the Palace of the Kings of Majorca in **Perpignan, Collioure**'s castle, the abbeys of **Saint-Michel-de-Cuxa** and **Saint-Martin-de-Canigou**, the **Priory of Serrabone** or the deeply-rooted Catalan traditions, from music (*coblas*), dance (*sardane*) and festivals (*Céret de Toros*, Céret's **Feria, Fête de l'Ours** the Bear Festival) to the maritime culture (fishing boats and cabins). **Perpignan** is the third largest city in Languedoc-Roussillon and promotes itself with its international *'Visa pour l'image' festi*val of photojournalism. Nevertheless the *département*'s sagging economy depends on the renewal of its ties with its Spanish cousins around Barcelona,[25] and Perpignan shows widening disparities between its retired population and its ethnic groups of Catalan gypsies and North-African immigrants.

In Perpignan, the municipal Charter for the Catalan language

La politique de promotion de la langue catalane n'est pas dirigée contre la langue française ... La politique linguistique en faveur du catalan est fondée sur l'incitation et l'encouragement, et non sur l'obligation ... La langue catalane est à la fois patrimoine et moyen d'expression de toute la population perpignanaise.[27]

The official promotion of the Catalan language does not pose a threat to the French language ... The linguistic programme to develop the study of the Catalan language believes in incentive and encouragement, not obligation ... The Catalan language is both an heritage and a means of expression for all the residents of Perpignan.

[Catalan is widely spoken beside French.]

The village skyline of Rivesaltes (Pyrénées-Orientales) Photo: Christian Saladin.

'El Canari', the little yellow train. Photo: Parc naturel régional des Pyrénées catalanes.

Le Petit Train Jaune — the Little Yellow Train

It took over twenty years to build the railway line linking **Villefranche-de-Conflent** to **Latour-de-Carol** in remote *Cerdagne*, one of the highest in Europe. It was abandoned with the opening of the road network, but *le Petit Train Jaune* was given a new lease of life thanks to tourism: *'El Canari'* ('the canary') offers unmatched mountain views and is an engineering feat.

Le Maréchal Joffre and the Joffre Museum,
Rivesaltes. Photos: Courtesy of Général
Cortale, Musée Joffre.

Rivesaltes and Joffre

Rivesaltes' most famous son gave his name to a street in practically all French towns: Joseph Joffre (1852-1931), from a family of local *vignerons*, was the general who won the first Battle of the Marne in September 1914, halting the German advance towards Paris. As commander-in-chief of the French and Allied armies, his reputation nevertheless became tarnished when he proved unable to end the stalemate of trench warfare, sacrificing huge numbers of men and ruthlessly getting rid of those he judged too 'soft'. He was relieved of his command in 1916, but was given the rank of marshal and performed only ceremonial roles thereafter (he also was elected to the *Académie française).*

General Joffre's order on 6 September 2014 is history :

Il importe de rappeler à tous que le moment n'est plus de regarder en arrière. (...) Une troupe qui ne peut plus avancer devra, coûte que coûte, garder le terrain conquis et se faire tuer sur place plutôt que de reculer. [28]

Everyone is to be reminded that this is no longer the time to look back. (...) Any troops stopped going forward must, at whatever cost, hold on to the conquered ground and be killed on the spot rather than retreat.

From 1938 to 1970, groups of 'undesirables' were detained in **Camp Joffre** in Rivesaltes, ranging from Spanish War Republican refugees, Jews and Gypsies bound for extermination camps, German prisoners of war, to Harkis (Algerian troops loyal to France during the Algerian War of Independence). This human tragedy under the sun awaits its memorial.[29]

L'homme sauvage - the legend of the wild man - and *la Fête de l'Ours* (Festival of the Bear)

The masquerades of the bear (*l'ours*) who becomes a man take place on three successive Sundays at *Chandeleur* (Candlemas, the Purification of the Virgin Mary) every February in **Prats-de-Mollo—La Preste, Saint-Laurent-de-Cerdans** and **Arles-sur-Tech**. These rituals reflect the legend that after their winter hibernation bears — associated with the Devil a long time ago — came down from the hills to look for maidens with whom to mate. [30]

> *Les ours, revêtus d'une peau de mouton ancestrale, reprennent vie. Noirs de suie, d'huile et de sueur, griffant et mordant ..., ils descendent ... accompagnés de leurs chasseurs. Ils marquent de leur empreinte tous ceux à leur portée, de préférence les jeunes filles. Lorsque le jour décline, les Barbiers, tout de blanc vêtus, les enchaînent ... et procèdent à un rasage symbolique.* [31]

> The bears [village young men], clad in ancestral lambskins, come alive. With their faces blackened with soot, oil and sweat, clawing and biting away, they come down, pursued by their hunters. They leave their mark on anybody within reach, preferably girls. By the end of the day, barbers, dressed in white, chain them up ... and proceed to give them a symbolic shave.

Thus an animal becomes a man — a 'wild man'.

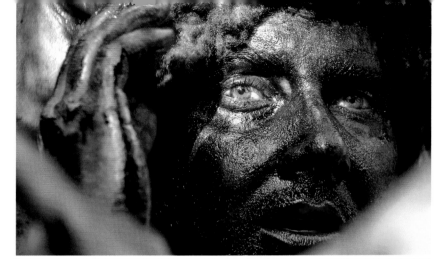

Fun and games at the Fête de l'Ours in Pyrénées-Orientales: a young man representing a wild man-bear with his face blackened by soot and grease; the wild men-bears are spotted bearing stout wooden poles; the march of the barbers dressed in white and carrying chains, axes and pieces of black pudding; a woman is captured by a wild man-bear; a 'bear' has been captured, chained up and ritually shaved by the barbers – note the black marks on the faces of the women in the crowd previously caught by the wild men-bears. Photos: Jacques Miot, Office de Tourisme, Prats-de-Mollo—La Preste.

VOICES OF LANGUEDOC-ROUSSILLON

Guiraud Riquier (1230-1292?), born in Narbonne (Aude), was called 'the last of the troubadours'. The northern lords who waged the Albigensian War (1208-1244) stamped out not only the Cathar heresy but also the refined poetic and musical tradition of the cultured South. The left column is in the original Occitan.

Serenada

Ad un fin aman fo datz	*A un amant fidèle*	To her devoted lover
Per si dons respiègs d'amor	*Sa dame lui donna un délai d'amour*	A lady gave a date
E'l sazos, e'l luecs mandatz.	*Fixant le temps et le lieu du rendez-vous.*	Telling him the time and the place.
E'l jorns,	*Et le jour où, le soir venu, il devait*	On the day when, at the coming of the evening,
qu'el ser dèc l'onor,	*Obtenir grand honneur,*	He would be granted high honour.
Penre, anava pessius,	*'ami s'en allait pensif*	Pensive the friend walked
E dizia sóspiran:	*Et disait en soupirant:*	And sighed, saying:
'Jorns, ben creisses a mon dan,	*'Jour, tu croîs à pour mon dommage,*	'Day, you harmed me as you dawned,
E'l sers auci'm	*Et le soir me tue*	Evening, you are killing me
E sos loncs espers.	*En me faisant si longtemps attendre.*	For you make me wait so long.

Bibliothèque nationale de France

Alphonse Daudet (1840-1897) was born in Nîmes (Gard) but is known as the most charming writer about Provence, where he purchased a windmill near Arles, after he had found fame in Paris. He was a poet, a playwright, and also wrote sensitive and realistic novels, though he is considered dated today (*Le Petit Chose* is largely autobiographical, *Tartarin de Tarascon, Le Nabab* are others). He is best remembered for his short stories (*Les Lettres de mon Moulin*, a tribute to Provence, and *Les Contes du lundi*, a patriotic tribute to France) which retain an everlasting freshness, stemming from simplicity, emotion and humour. As a story-teller, he created immortal characters who are an integral part of French culture, familiar to all ages: Monsieur Seguin's wayward but brave little goat that came to a tragic end because of its disobedience; the beautiful and deadly '*Arlésienne*' whom nobody ever gets to see — a Provençal *femme fatale* who inspired the composer Georges Bizet to write his opera of the same name; *Révérend Père Gaucher* who concocts a wonderful liqueur to save his monastery from bankruptcy, but pushes the necessary tasting a bit too far, with the forgiveness of his market-driven brothers; *Tartarin de Tarascon*, the epitome of the southern braggart.

The picturesque village of Cucugnan (Aude). Photo: Mairie de Cucugnan.

Le Curé de Cucugnan

'L'abbé Martin était curé de Cucugnan. Bon comme le pain, franc comme l'or, il aimait paternellement ses Cucugnanais ... Mais hélas! Les araignées filaient dans son confessionnal et, le beau jour de Pâques, les hosties restaient au fond de son saint ciboire. Un dimanche, Monsieur Martin monta en chaire.'

'Father Martin was Cucugnan's priest. He had a heart of gold, he was trustworthy and he loved his Cucugnanais dearly, like a good father. Alas! Spiders were spinning webs in his confessional and, on fair Easter day, the bread (hosts) would remain at the bottom of his holy ciborium. One Sunday, Monsieur Martin ascended his pulpit.'

[Worried sick about his parishioners' souls, he dreams up a stratagem to convince them to become more faithful.]

'Mes frères,' dit-il,' vous me croirez si vous voulez ; l'autre nuit, je me suis trouvé à la porte du paradis.

Je frappai : saint Pierre m'ouvrit!

«Tiens ! C'est vous, mon brave Monsieur Martin, » me fit-il ; » quel bon vent ?...et qu'y a-t-il pour votre service? »

«Beau saint Pierre, vous qui tenez le grand livre et la clef, pourriez-vous me dire, si je ne suis pas trop curieux, combien vous avez de Cucugnanais en paradis ? »

'Saint Pierre prit son gros livre, l'ouvrit et mit ses besicles:'

«Voyons un peu: Cucugnan, disons-nous. Cu...Cu...Cucugnan. Nous y sommes. Mon brave Monsieur Martin, la page est toute blanche. Pas une âme. Pas plus de Cucugnanais que d'arêtes dans une dinde. »

[The Purgatory angel is next:] « Eh ! Saint homme, ils sont en paradis. Où diantre voulez-vous qu'ils soient? »

«Mais j'en viens, du paradis! »

«Vous en venez ? Eh bien ? »

« Eh bien ! Ils n'y sont pas ! Ah ! Bonne mère des anges! »

« Que voulez-vous, Monsieur le curé ! S'ils ne sont ni en paradis, ni en purgatoire, il n'y a pas de milieu, ils sont ... »

'Jésus! Marie! Joseph! Personne de Cucugnan en purgatoire! Où sont-ils donc?'

[Mustering his courage, he gives one last try at the gates of Hell. The Devil promptly informs him:]

"Ah! Feu de Dieu! Tu fais la bête, toi, comme si tu ne savais pas que tout Cucugnan est ici!" '

'My dear brothers,' he started, 'believe me if you will, but during the past night, I found myself at Heaven's gate. I knocked: Saint Peter himself came to open the door!'

«What a surprise! So it is you, my good Monsieur Martin," he said. "What brings you here? What can I do for you?"

"Your Lordship Saint Peter, you who are the keeper of the big Register and the Key, could you tell me, begging your pardon if I am too nosy, how many Cucugnan residents you have in Heaven?"

'Saint Peter took his big book, opened it and put on his spectacles:'

"Let's see: Cucugnan, we said. Cu...Cu...Cucugnan. Here we are. My dear Monsieur Martin, the page is completely blank, I am afraid. Not a soul. No more Cucugnanais than there are fishbones in a turkey."

[Even more worried, the good priest tries his luck in Purgatory: the answer is identical, none of his parishioners is there.]

'Jesus! Mary! Joseph! No one from Cucugnan in Purgatory! Where on earth could they be?'

[The Purgatory angel:]   "Come on, holy man, they are in Heaven. Seriously, where would you want them to be?"

"The problem is, I have just come back from Heaven!"

"So you have! Well?"

"Well, they are not there!"

"Dear me! Holy Mother of the angels!" "Listen, my good priest, if they are neither in Heaven nor in Purgatory, you've got to come to your senses: the only other alternative is ..."

[Mustering his courage, he gives one last try at the gates of Hell. The Devil promptly informs him:]

"What is this, by the Hell fire! You dare to joke with me, stupid fool, as if you did not know that the whole village of Cucugnan is here indeed!" '

[To his terrified flock, the priest prescribes the only path to salvation: general confession. Soon, the Cucugnanais turn into model parishioners.]

La Légende du Babau

This is one of the best-loved legends in southern France. The villainous monster's name is sometimes spelled 'Babaou', depending on local pronunciation. The version below is shared with us by the people of Rivesaltes (Pyrénées-Orientales).

'Il était une fois, un petit village du nom de Rivesaltes, bien paisible derrière ses remparts ... La nuit sans lune du 2 février 1290, alors que tout le monde dort d'un profond sommeil, un vacarme épouvantable retentit ... Six bébés viennent de disparaître, enlevés par une bête énorme entrée par le Forat del forn (le Trou du four), par lequel on jette d'ordinaire cendres et déchets. Une autre nuit, le veilleur du village aperçoit ... une sorte d'iguane à la mâchoire redoutable et aux griffes impressionnantes. Quand le Batlle (le maire) demande une description de l'animal, l'homme, devenu bègue de frayeur, ne peut qu'articuler, « va...vau », c'est-à-dire « il a...il a ». C'est ainsi que «va vau» se transforma en «Ba bau».'

L'affaire n'avait que trop duré. En 1290, l'homme de la situation est sans nul doute Galdric Trencaven, seigneur des Fraisses et Périllos. C'est un habile arbalétrier. Il suspend des cochons aux remparts pour appâter la bête sanguinaire. Dans une maison voisine, en tenue de combat, il se tient prêt ... Au bout de la quatrième nuit, Trencaven put enfin décocher deux flèches mortelles dans la gorge de l'animal. Le monstre était enfin terrassé. La population fêta dignement, par une messe et un banquet mémorable, la fin de ce terrible drame.'

'Once upon a time, there was a small village named Rivesaltes, nice and comfortable behind its walls. On the moonless night of 2nd February 1290, while everyone was fast asleep, a horrible tumult rang out. Six babies had just disappeared, snatched away by a huge beast who had gained access through the Forat del forn (the oven hole), normally used to dump ashes and refuse. On another night, the village watchman caught sight of a kind of iguana, with deadly jaws and dreadful claws. When the Batlle (the Mayor) asked him to describe the animal, the man was so frightened that he could only stammer, "va ... vau", which means "it has ... it has". That is how "va vau" was changed into "Ba bau".

The situation could not be tolerated any longer. In 1290, the only man capable of rising to the challenge is without doubt Galdric Trencaven, Lord of Fraisses and Perillos. He is a skilfull marksman. He hangs pigs on the walls to lure the bloodthirsty beast. Hiding inside a neighbouring house, dressed for combat, he is ready. On the fourth night, Trencaven was finally able to shoot two mortal arrows into the animal's throat. The monster had been slain, at last. The population celebrated properly the end of that awful tragedy, with a mass and a memorable banquet.'

[According to Monsieur Christian Saladin, who kindly communicated the tale, one of Babau's ribs can still be seen in Rivesaltes *Office Municipal d'Animation et de Tourisme!*]

Bibliothèque Nationale de France

André Chamson (1900-1983), pictured here in his Academician's outfit, was a native of Nîmes (Gard) like Alphonse Daudet, and a graduate of the venerable *Ecole des Chartes* in Paris (www.enc.sorbonne.fr). He had a long career as an archivist and museum curator before becoming the Director of the Archives de France. He was a poet and author, which led to his being elected to the *Académie française*. His roots were in the *Cévennes* of his forefathers, and his novels — *Roux le bandit, L'Auberge de l'abîme, La neige et la fleur, Suite cévenole*, for example — were set in that harsh countryside. True to his religious tradition, he led the annual Protestant commemoration of *L'Assemblée du Désert* seven times, and devoted fourteen years of his life to the evocation of the *Guerre des Camisards* (*La Tour de Constance, Castanet, le Camisard de l'Aigoual ...*). One of his books, *Catinat*, tells the story of Abdias Maurel, the young and herculean *Camargue gardian* [mounted herdsman in charge of bulls or horses; the herds were called *manades*] who headed the *Camisard* cavalry. As a *résistant* like many of his countrymen, he headed the Alsace-Lorraine division with André Malraux. Chamson's grave is not in a cemetery, but in a natural setting facing the Cévennes mountains at Serre de la Luzette in Vallenaugues, an exceptional privilege.

Le côté essentiellement montagnard des Enfants de Dieu fait que l'histoire n'a pas tenu grand compte des cavaliers qu'il y avait parmi eux. Il apportaient pourtant une aide considérable ... 'Tue, tue! Vive l'épée de Gédéon! Vive l'épée de l'Eternel! Quand il pensait au temple de sa région, détruit par le fer et par le feu, Catinat entrait dans une colère sacrée. Il démolissait les églises des prêtres comme on avait démoli les temples de ses pasteurs ... Comme armement, Catinat et ses compagnons emportaient d'ordinaire avec eux leur pique de travail qu'ils désignaient indifféremment comme 'lou ferre' ou 'lou fichaïroun' dans la langue du pays. C'est avec cette pique qu'ils faisaient obéir les taureaux mais, pour les expéditions lointaines, ils glissaient deux pistolets dans les fontes de leurs selles ... et dans le revers de leurs bottes, ils enfonçaient toujours un couteau à longue lame tranchante des deux côtés. Les chevaux qu'ils montaient ... crinières longues et blanches que chaque cavalier avait la coquetterie de bien peigner, la queue fouettante, étaient capables de passer partout, en particulier sur le bord des roubines, ces canaux d'eau morte qui dessinent comme un damier dangereux à travers toute la Petite Camargue.

The Children of God [the *Camisards*] were mostly mountain people, which explains why history did not say much about these horsemen. Yet, their help was essential ... 'Kill, kill! Hail the sword of Gedeon! Hail the sword of the Eternal!' Whenever Catinat thought of the temple [Protestant church] in his land, destroyed by iron and fire ... a holy anger would take hold of him. He would pull down the priests' [Catholic] churches the same way his pastors' temples had been pulled down ... For weapons, Catinat and his companions usually brought with them their long work pikes, which they would call either *'lou ferre'* or *'lou fichaïroun'* in the language of their country. Such a pike was used to force the bulls to obey but, for distant expeditions, they would slip two pistols in the holsters of their saddles and, inside the top of their boots, they would always stick a knife with a sharp double-edged blade. The horses they were riding ... with skilfully combed long white manes that were the pride of each rider, their swishing tails, could thread their way anywhere, especially along the edge of *roubines*, those stagnant water canals which form a perilous checkerboard all across *Petite Camargue* [right bank of the Rhône delta).

[Catinat was the last *Camisard* leader to be taken by the king's troops in April 1705. He was burned at the stake in Nîmes. *'Plusieurs conseillers voulaient que Catinat fut tiré à quatre chevaux, mais le plus grand nombre opina pour le feu, parce que, disait-on, le feu est un supplice plus violent et plus long que le déchirement.'* ('Several judges wanted Catinat to be pulled apart by four horses, but the majority opted for the stake because, as they would say, fire is a more violent and longer torture than quartering.')]

Charles Trenet. Photo: alain.ferrand.com

Charles Trenet (1913-2001), who called himself *"le fou chantant"* (the Singing Madman), was a native of Narbonne (Aude). His long and legendary singing career took off like a rocket in 1938 after he had been noticed by the great Maurice Chevalier. The straw-haired Charles was booked to appear at the beginning of the first part of a show. Dressed in Mediterranean elegance — cobalt blue shirt and suit (to match his eyes), white tie, a flower in his buttonhole, light grey hat — he started singing. He was supposed to sing three numbers, but ended up singing twelve! He wrote every single line of his songs, all bursting with a poetic *joie de vivre*.

La Mer

[No fewer than 400 versions of this song exist: a timeless piece repeated everywhere in the world.]

La mer	The sea
Qu'on voit danser le long des golfes clairs	That you can see dancing along the bright bays
A des reflets d'argent	Has silver reflections
La mer	The sea
Des reflets changeants	Changing reflections
Sous la pluie	Under the rain
La mer	The sea
Au ciel d'été confond	In the summer sky
Ses blancs moutons	Her 'white horses' [appear]
Avec les anges si purs	As angels so pure
La mer bergère d'azur	The sea azure-clad shepherdess
Infinie	Infinite
La mer	The sea
A bercé mon cœur pour la vie	Has cradled my heart for ever

[Note: There is no punctuation for this song as is the case for some poems. The song was actually scribbled by Trenet on a piece of paper while on board a train.]

Jean Lartéguy (1920-2011) was born Jean-Pierre Osty in Maisons-Alfort (Val-de-Marne), in the Ile-de-France region but his family was from Lozère. All his life, he was a fighter and a soldier involved in all the conflicts of the second half of the twentieth century. He went off to war aged 19, became a commando officer of the French Free Forces during the Second World War, and then served in the Korean War, the Indochinese War and the Algerian War. As a war correspondent and journalist for *Paris-Match*, he witnessed all the other crises which affected the world, from Latin America to Africa and Palestine, and was awarded the prestigious *Prix Albert-Londres* for journalism in 1955. Having put his first-hand experience into a series of military novels, he became a legend with his international best-seller, *Les Centurions* (1960), plunging into the depths of French Indochina and Algeria in the throes of war. Lartéguy exposed cowardly politicians and warned that the time had come for dealing with unconventional warfare and developing counter-insurgency strategies focusing on psychology. The French never gave him any literary prize but some American commanders during the Iraq and Afghanistan Wars were inspired by reading his *Centurions*. He had the privilege to spend his last days in the Invalides, the military hospital in Paris.

In *Les Baladins de la Margeride*, Lartéguy tells of his formative years. He starts with the portrait of his grand-mother, in the village of Aumont-Aubrac (Lozère):

Ma grand-mère, la Vieille, arriva le lendemain (de ma naissance), m'enroula dans son fichu et m'emporta au fond des montagnes de la Margeride. J'étais le premier mâle de ses petits-enfants: je devais pousser sur le sol rocailleux où notre famille s'accrochait depuis des siècles. La Vieille portait la coiffe noire, elle n'avait pas de sac, mais, comme les religieuses, d'immenses poches où des croûtons de pain voisinaient avec un rosaire, un mouchoir à carreaux et un vieux couteau Laguiole qui était celui de mon grand-père. Ce couteau était le signe de la royauté des maîtres de ferme. Quand le maître s'assoit à table et ouvre son couteau, les domestiques qui partagent son repas commencent à rompre le pain ; quand il le ferme en faisant claquer, tous se lèvent. Les femmes se tiennent debout près de l'âtre, leur bol à la main. Quand elle devint veuve, la Vieille mangea à la table des hommes et claqua le couteau.

My grandmother, the Old Lady, came the following day (after my birth), wrapped me in her shawl and took me away to the heart of the *Margeride* mountains. I was her first male grandchild: I had to grow up on the rocky soil to which my family had been clinging for centuries. The Old Lady wore the black *coiffe*, she did not have a purse, but, like the nuns, huge pockets which contained bread crusts as well as a rosary, a checked handkerchief and an old *Laguiole* knife which was my grand-father's. This knife was the symbol of a landlord's authority. When the farmer sits down at the table and opens his knife, the servants who share his meal start breaking the bread; when he closes it with a loud snap, everyone rises. The women remain standing by the hearth, with bowl in hand. When she became a widow, the Old Lady ate at the men's table and snapped her knife shut.

Reprinted with kind permission of Editions Albin Michel, Paris. Translation by Catherine Pinchetti.

The Margeride near Châteauneuf-de-Randon (Lozère). Photo: E. Debenne.

Bibliographic references

1   *Le Midi libre*, éd. de Narbonne, 15/12/2010

2   www.midilibre.fr, 12/04/2012

3   *Le Point*, n° 2130, *11 juillet 2013*

4   *Viaduc Magazine*, n° 4 (novembre 2004)

5   *Bulletin municipal de Cap d'Agde (été* 2011*)*

6   www.midilibre.fr, 31 août 2014 (anti-corrida demonstration in Carcassonne)

7   *Viaduc Magazine, ibid.*

8   *Le Journal du rugby*, mai 2012

9   BRUALLA, Christian. *100 ans de passion, histoire du rugby biterrois*. Béziers : ASBH, 2011. (See also : www.asbh.net)

10 CARTIER, Jean-Pierre. *Histoire de la croisade contre les Albigeois*. Paris, Editions Bernard Grasset, 1968.

11 *Le Midi libre*, 12/12/2010

12 www.laregion-culture.fr

13 www.montpellier-agglo.com

14 www.museedudesert.com

15 www.lemonde.fr (« Lifestyle »), 13/07/2010

16 BOILEAU (Pierre), NARCEJAC (Thomas). *Dans la gueule du loup*. Paris : Gallimard Jeunesse, Folio Junior n° 847, 2009.

17 *Lozère nouvelle*, 22/07/2011

18 www.polen-mende.com

19 *Inscription 'Devoir de mémoire'* on Maquis Montaigne Stele, Col de l'Exil, Lozère

20 Extract from his lecture '*Inspirations méditerranéennes' in Paris, 1934 ; see www.agora.qc.ca/Dossiers/Paul_Valery*

21 www.winetourisminfrance.com, *Les Cépages oubliés ont de l'avenir*, 10/02/2011

22 www.1.montpellier.inra.fr/vassal/

23 *Viaduc Magazine*, ibid.

24   *Vent Sud Magazine, juillet* 2005

25   www.lindependant.fr, 22 juin 2014 (on *'La Première bulle'*)

26   *L'Express, 'Fiers d'être catalans'*, 11/05/2011

27   *Journal municipal de Perpignan, janvier* 2012

28   General Joffre as quoted in : LE NAOUR, Jean-Yves. *1914 : La Grande illusion.* Paris : Perrin, 2012.

29   www.cg66.fr (Mémorial de Rivesaltes)

30   FREGER, Charles, *Wilder Mann – the Image of the Savage.* Dewi Lewis Publishing, Stockport. Reprinted 2014.

31   www.lasemaineduroussillon.com, (Sebastià Vilanou y Poncet), 27 février 2014

Voices of Languedoc-Roussillon

BEC, Pierre. *Nouvelle Anthologie de la lyrique occitane du Moyen-Age.* Avignon : Aubanel, 1970.

DAUDET, Alphonse. *Les Lettres de mon moulin.* Paris : Gallimard, Folio Junior, 1990.

La Légende du Babau, Office municipal d'Animation et deTourisme de Rivesaltes (Pyrénées-Orientales), M. SALADIN Christian.

CHAMSON, André. *Catinat, gardian de Camargue, chef de la cavalerie Camisarde.* Paris : Plon, 1982.

TRENET, Charles, *La Mer.* www.paroles2chanson.com.

LARTEGUY, Jean. *Les Baladins de la Margeride.* Paris : Presses Pocket, 1962.

Not to be missed

Villes et Pays d'Art et d'Histoire

Nîmes, Uzès (Gard); Mende, Lot-en-Gévaudan (Lozère); Pézenas (Hérault); Narbonne (Aude); Perpignan, Vallée de la Têt (Pyrénées-Orientales).

Plus Beaux Détours de France

Marvejols (Lozère); Lodève, Pézenas (Hérault); Limoux (Aude); Prades (Pyrénées-Orientales).

Plus Beaux Villages de France
Aiguèze (Gard); La Garde-Guérin, Sainte-Enimie (Lozère); Minerve, Olargues, Saint-Guilhem-le-Désert (Hérault); Lagrasse (Aude); Castelnou, Eus, Mosset, Villefranche-de-Conflent (Pyrénées-Orientales).

Parc national des Causses-Cévennes (UNESCO), **Parcs naturels régionaux** du Haut-Languedoc, de la Narbonnaise en Méditerranée, des Pyrénées catalanes.

UNESCO World Heritage Sites: Pont du Gard (Gard); *Parc national des Causses-Cévennes* (Gard, Lozère); Canal du Midi (Hérault, Aude): Carcassonne (Aude); *Chemins de Compostelle – Via Tolosana*, sites at Saint-Gilles-du-Gard (Gard), Pont du Diable and Saint-Guilhem-le-Désert (Hérault); Vauban fortifications, sites at Villefranche-de-Conflent and Mont-Louis (Pyrénées-Orientales).

Regional Websites
www.cr-languedoc-roussillon.fr
www.sunfrance.com
www.tourismegard.com
www.uzes.fr
www.ville-aigues-mortes.fr
www.causses-et-cevennes.org
www.lozere-tourisme.com
www.ville-marvejols.fr
www.herault-tourisme.com
www.ville-agde.fr
www.aude.fr
www.audecathare.fr
www.ville-castelnaudary.fr
www.cg66.fr
www.mairie-rivesaltes.fr
www.parc-pyrenees-catalanes.fr

Regional Newspapers
Le Midi libre, www.midilibre.fr,
L'Indépendant, www.lindependant.fr.

Universities
Montpellier: www.univ-montp1.fr, www.univ-montp2.fr, www.univ-montp3.fr,
Perpignan: www.univ-perp.fr.

Regional acknowledgements

Our warmest thanks go to the following contributors who kindly shared with us photographs illustrating their region:

GARD

AIGUES-MORTES: Groupe Salins (former Salins du Midi), M. Antoine JULE, Communication.

ALÈS: Mairie, M. Jacques SCUDERI, Photothèque.

UZÈS: Comité départemental du Tourisme du Gard, Mme Dominique ANDRÉ.

LOZÈRE

FAU-DE-PEYRE: Mairie, M. Daniel MANTRAND, Maire de Fau-de-Peyre.

MARVEJOLS: Mairie, M. Jean-François DELOUSTAL, Maire de Marvejols.

MENDE : Comité départemental du Tourisme de la Lozère, Mme Caroline VIDAL-SALS, Manager Opérationnel des Pôles 'Promotion Générale' et 'Ingénierie-Qualité'.

HÉRAULT

AGDE: Hôtel de Ville, M. Laurent UROZ, Service de la Communication.

MARSEILLAN : Office de tourisme de Marseillan, Mme Afrae EL HADRAMI, Responsable.

MONTAGNAC: Domaines viticoles Paul Mas, Mme Julie BILLOD.

PÉZENAS : Office de Tourisme de Pézenas-Val-d'Hérault, Mme Marie-Pierre PONTOIS

AUDE

CASTELNAUDARY: Mairie, Mme Audrey GODIN, Service Communication.

CUCUGNAN: Théâtre Achille-Mir, Mmes Elisabeth ROUVIÈRE et Véronique MEAUX, Service Communication et animations.

NARBONNE (Château L'Hospitalet): Vins Gérard Bertrand, Mmes Véronique BRAUN et Chloé FUCHS, Service de la Communication.

PYRÉNÉES-ORIENTALES

CANET-en-ROUSSILLON : Mairie, Mme Audrey ANDONEGUI, Direction de la Communication.

MONT-LOUIS : Syndicat mixte du Parc naturel régional des Pyrénées Catalanes, Mme Véronique DAUMONT, chargée de Communication

PERPIGNAN : Comité Interprofessionnel des Vins du Roussillon (CIVR), Mme Christiane COUANAU, Photothèque.

PORT-VENDRES : Conseil Général des Pyrénées-Orientales, M. Samuel VILLEVIEILLE, Atelier des Barques, Site de Paulilles.

PRATS-DE-MOLLO—LA-PRESTE : Office de Tourisme, Mme Any CAPELL, Responsable Accueil-Animatrice Numérique du Territoire; Photographe, M. Jacques MIOT.

RIVESALTES: Office de Tourisme de Rivesaltes, M. Christian SALADIN, Photothèque.

Musée du Maréchal Joffre ; we are especially grateful to Général CORTALE, Président du Comité du Musée du Maréchal Joffre, who selected the photographs, and to Georges FERNANDEZ.

Barques catalanes, distinctive small regional sailing-boats.
Photo: © M. Castillo, Atelier des barques, Paulilles; courtesy Samuel Villevieille,
Conseil Général des Pyrénées-Orientales.

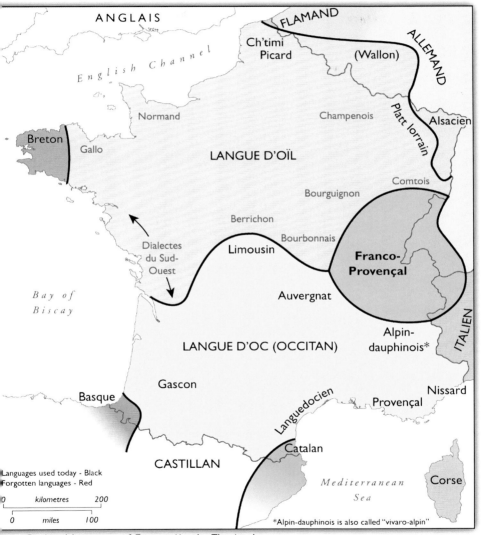

Regional languages of France. Map by Tim Aspden.

Index

The beach at Le Canet. Photo: Ville de Canet-en-Roussillon.

Biography

Parisian-born **Catherine Pinchetti** is a graduate of the *École Nationale des Chartes*, a French *Grande École* for historians and curators of heritage subjects. She built up an extensive and rich experience teaching French as a foreign language in the United States (Vermont, New York State, and Washington DC), in France (Fontainebleau) and the United Kingdom (Cambridge). She taught in prep schools, universities, *Alliances Françaises* and Chambers of Commerce. She also contributed numerous articles in *Bien-dire*, a French magazine for learners of French, and in *Go! English*, a similar journal for learners of English. She was actively involved in fostering cross-Channel language and cultural exchanges, notably through twinning associations and summer job-placements for students. She now divides her time between Cambridge and Fontainebleau, and has embarked on a new career as a writer.